TECHNIQUE AND STYLE
IN CHORAL SINGING

by
GEORGE HOWERTON
Dean, School of Music
Northwestern University

$5.00

CARL FISCHER
INC.
62 Cooper Square, New York 3
BOSTON • CHICAGO • DALLAS •

3867

CONTENTS

iii

N2584

PREFACE

THE writing of a book on choral technique was prompted by the inquiries of choral directors, former choristers and students as to how one sets about developing good choral performance. The attempt has been made to evolve a set of principles based upon the experiences encountered in training amateur singers for public performances of various types—church services, concerts of sacred and secular music and television and radio performances by school and church choirs, concert presentations of choral-orchestral works from the symphonic repertoire under such conductors as Bruno Walter, Pierre Monteux, William Steinberg, Rafael Kubelik, Otto Klemperer, Fritz Reiner, Désiré Defauw and others.

If this book provides some assistance to the choral director in bringing about a type of singing that is effective to the audience, satisfying to the singer and esthetically significant, it will go a long way toward serving the purpose for which it is intended.

Appreciation is expressed to Dr. John Samuel Kenyon for advice in the area of diction, to Dr. Curt R. Goedsche for assistance in matters relating to the German language, to Jean Kaufman and Louise Evans for bibliographical aid, and to Anne Williams for her work in the preparation of the typescript.

Evanston, Illinois   George Howerton
October first, 1956

v

PART ONE

Technique

N 2584

CHAPTER I

SINGING – A SYNTHESIS OF HABITS

The purpose of choral singing should be to provide a means of self-expression through contact with the great masterpieces of the literature. Singing with others music of no matter what quality can produce a type of joy peculiar to itself. When the music is good, the result is an experience esthetically meaningful; when the performance is characterized not only by the joy of the singer in producing, but also by excellence of presentation for the gratification of the listener, it will have attained the quality of a significant art expression.

To make possible a meaningful and effective presentation of the literature, a well-established technique is prerequisite. Consequently, the conductor who is interested in fine performance must direct attention to the development in the group of a habit of singing that will set forth each composition with the greatest artistry and musical skill of which the organization may be capable.

Singing is an activity made up of many separate elements. It may be called a process of synthesis, in which a number of individual components enter to make a total response. A singer's effectiveness largely depends upon the degree to which he is able to combine these diversified constituents into one unified reaction. If any particular factor is overemphasized or given undue importance, the singing becomes distorted and ill-proportioned. If some one aspect is neglected or given insufficient attention, the singing becomes ineffectual, weak, and unconvincing. The various components should constitute a set of reactions so firmly fixed that they automatically come into play whenever the individual begins to sing. As long as the singer must give conscious attention to any one of the separate aspects of the singing process, he is unable to achieve a performance that is fully rounded and complete.

1

First of all, the student must become aware of the various factors involved. Secondly, he not only must be aware of the separate integrants but must strive from the beginning to develop them concomitantly. If for a time he concentrates upon one aspect with the idea that after he has achieved mastery of it he will proceed to the next, he will find himself in a dilemma. As he studies the first specific element, he will discover that mastery in any one area is not quickly or easily achieved. So much time may be spent in seeking it that none is left for the solution of other problems equally or even more important. For instance, if a singer is determined to attain perfection in tone production before attacking another problem, he quite likely may have set for himself an impossible goal. Tone production as such seldom satisfies one completely; there is usually some additional refinement to be made. If one concentrates intensively upon production, it is easy to become so preoccupied with it that other factors are ignored.

For example, diction may be sacrificed to quality. There are many performers who sing with exquisite tone, but whose words are incomprehensible. On the other hand, there are those who give such extreme and exclusive care to the enunciation of text that all considerations of tonal beauty seem to have escaped them. Skillful and artistic singing calls for a delicate balance between the two elements. It requires that the tone be characterized by physical beauty, but that, at the same time, the text be projected with clarity and understanding.

As a further illustration, the mere achievement of breath control can become a matter for exclusive concentration, in fact a fetish. Breath control has no immediate value in itself. Yet instructors often devote themselves solely to this problem in the earlier stages of training. Breath control is valuable only when utilized in the production of tone, when it supplies the means of giving resonance and brilliance, when it provides the strength necessary for audibility, when it makes possible the singing of the musical phrase in its unbroken entirety. In other words, breath control is important only when it becomes part of an activity involving the synthesis of several elements.

So with all the factors involved in the process of singing. Each has its role to play and must have its proper development. Each, however, must be developed in relation to the others, and the various integrants must be developed simultaneously.

It should be the intent of every instructor of singing, whether private teacher or choral director, so to train his students that, no matter when or where they sing, they will have developed for themselves a set of habits that will enable them always to sing to the full extent of their capabilities. Furthermore, it should be his intent so to equip them that when they leave his tutelage and no longer have the benefit of his instruction they will take with them a technique that will continue to serve in good stead.

The personal inspiration of the teacher is important, but dependence upon it often has been overemphasized. Too many singing organizations perform beautifully under a particular director but without him produce only mediocre results. The excellent performance of the m o m e n t is not enough, no matter how good it may be. The truly wise instructor is the one who sets for himself, not the ideal of training singers to perform beautifully while under his direction, but rather that of sending out students who will have such understanding of the singing process and such vocal equipment that whatever singing they do will always be meaningful and effective.

The attainment of excellence in public performance is an important part of the training process. However, it should not be stressed to the degree that it becomes a total end in itself. The concert provides pleasure for the student, for the conductor, and, it is to be hoped, for the audience as well. However, it should become something more than an effective sequence of selections well performed; it should also act as an impetus to continued study. Public performance can become so much the end and aim of instruction that nothing lasts beyond it, but unless in the course of working upon the presentation proper skills and habits are developed, unless the individual carries to the next performance something more of understanding and of skill than was his before, it cannot be said to have justified itself.

Accordingly, in setting out to train a choral group, the director should attempt to lay slowly and deliberately, but nonetheless firmly, the foundation for a structure of technique. It is difficult to be content with such an approach. The immediate impulse is to prepare material for public presentation, to get the singers started directly on the first program of the season. However, the conductor will achieve more lasting results if he will content himself with a procedure that may possibly get into motion more slowly but will eventually result in greater speed and efficiency.

Let the singers embark upon a concert program, working upon actual musical material for presentation, but let them realize that in preparing the program they are to establish the foundations for a technique that not only will serve for the immediate present but will carry over into the future as well. They should realize that the development of this technique will facilitate the preparation of subsequent programs, enabling them to learn more material and material of greater difficulty and, at the same time, to learn it more quickly.

It is comparatively easy for the skillful director to take a group of singers, even raw recruits with little ability, and by using a strictly imitative approach turn out a good program in short order. It takes a great deal more skill, plus a high degree of imagination, for a director to plan the first performance so that it will be not only an effective presentation in itself, but also a means of advancing his singers in proficiency as musically intelligent beings.

In using the imitative approach the director merely points out the weak passages, indicating actual mistakes that have been made and attending to their immediate rectification. He sees to it that the faults are removed, but does not proceed beyond this point. As a consequence, the rehearsal time is devoted to nothing beyond the actual preparation of the selections. As a rule, the first concert can be prepared fairly quickly through this technique. On the other hand, the singers have made no attempt to analyze the difficulties encountered nor devoted any effort toward an attempt to comprehend the underlying causes. Therefore, they do not know how to avoid like errors in the future, and the next time similar problems arise, the identical errors are likely to be repeated.

If the director can lay his finger on the basic weakness in a particular passage and can briefly indicate its cause, he is taking a step toward establishing basic habits. Suppose, for example, that the group is misreading, as singers often do, the rhythmic pattern involving the subdivision of the quarter-note into a group of two eighth-notes. Most persons have a tendency to sing the ♪ ♪ pattern as though it were the ♪. ♪ pattern. It is comparatively easy for the director to say, "That is wrong, sing it this way," and then illustrate the correct method of performance, either by singing the figure or by having the accompanist play it. A procedure yielding more enduring benefits would be for the director to stop and say, "Note the passage on page so-and-so at such-and-such a measure. You are misreading the pattern of two eighth-notes as though it were a dotted eighth followed by a sixteenth." If he then were to write on a blackboard (which should be at hand for all rehearsals) the pattern of the dotted eighth followed by a sixteenth, he could give the group both a visual and an aural idea of the difference between the two. If he were to have the group sing the two patterns several times while he pointed to the board, attention could be focused on the proper manner of performance and also on the incorrect one previously employed.

It should be impressed upon the singers that the error in question is a common one. It should be stressed that the singer who is musically alert will always be on the lookout for this particular pattern and will take care that each note is given proper value. A further step in the development of this aspect of technique would be to examine all points in the selection where the quarter-note is so subdivided. Specific exercises could be developed by drilling the group on every such passage. Any group which becomes aware of the difficulty and alert to surmount it is evolving its own singing technique rather than blindly following the director's instructions of the moment.

The above is admittedly a slower procedure than the imitative one but it will prove to be economical of rehearsal time in the long run. Thereafter, if a similar error occurs, the director has merely to point it out with the expectation that the group will be able to correct it without further discussion. As time goes on, and as attention is called to this type of error, the group eventually will develop the habit of noting the subdivision and of singing it correctly without comment from the director.

When the singer ultimately realizes that the basic problem in approaching new music is not that of learning the correct notes and then applying to them what he usually thinks of as "expression" or "interpretation," but is rather that of noting basic problems, of giving attention to phrase contour, relative time-values, pitch relationships and appropriate dynamic schemes, he is beginning to develop the synthesis of activity that good singing demands. When he combines with this the automatic support of adequately controlled breath and the procedures insuring good tone quality and production, he is on the way to becoming a creative singer in his own right.

CHAPTER II

POSTURE AND BREATHING; MUSCULAR ARTICULATION

In building up a synthesis of proper singing habits, attention should first be directed toward the matter of physical preparation. Here one may consider those factors which bear upon the production of tone quality as affected by the action of the body mechanism. Such considerations as posture, breath support, articulation of tongue, lips, and jaw, and freedom of activity on the part of the throat muscles, the head, and the arms are important in determining tonal quality. These are not the only factors involved, but they are basic in achieving good production.

In a proper sitting attitude, the body will be erect and firm at all times. The trunk must be straight so that the breath may be supplied from the diaphragm to the resonating cavities without interference. In standing, the weight should be balanced easily and comfortably on the feet. Singers usually will find themselves most comfortable if the feet are slightly apart with one foot perhaps somewhat in advance of the other. The muscles of the legs and the trunk should be flexed, and in a proper state of tension.

"A proper state of tension" may be described as one in which the body is ready for active physical movement, but sufficiently relaxed for that movement to be free and unimpeded. The muscular apparatus should be resilient, firm but not rigid: the chest and shoulders should be held normally high, without undue effort, but in such a position as to suggest vitality. The head should be erect, balanced lightly but firmly so that the singer can move his head freely, with no sensation of binding in the neck muscles. The arms should be relaxed; the hands may be dropped easily at the sides and the arms allowed to hang freely from the shoulders, or the hands may be lightly clasped together in front of the singer at a point slightly above the waistline. When this latter position is used, care should be exercised to see that

7

the elbows are not pressed against the sides in such a manner that undue constriction ensues.

In a sitting position, the singer should balance himself comfortably, with the hips pushed toward the back of the chair. The feet should be planted firmly on the floor, with the weight distributed between hips and feet as if balanced between those points. Many singers when seated have a tendency to collapse the bodily structure toward the hips so that the abdominal muscles are crowded together. It is in order to avoid this constriction that the singer is instructed to carry the weight to the feet, maintaining the trunk in a generally upright position, but with the body inclined slightly forward. It will usually be necessary for the singer to sit somewhat forward in the chair, at the same time directing the weight of the hips toward the back of the chair. As in standing, it may be more comfortable for the feet to be slightly apart, with one foot in advance of the other.

It is often helpful to think of the bodily structure as a framework, the foundation planted firmly on the ground, the structure reaching to its greatest height—which is another way of saying that the head and shoulders should be held high. The idea of "hanging the weight from the shoulders," of thinking of the shoulders as a beam, will often prove effective in bringing the necessary resilience into the body. The singers must be impressed with the necessity for the maintenance of constant vitality in the physical attitude and should become accustomed to singing either sitting or standing.

With a beginning group which is seated the following procedures may be helpful:

a. The singers are asked to "push the hips as far back in the chair as possible."
b. They are requested to "place the feet firmly on the floor."
c. They are next told to "throw the weight forward to the feet."

d. The group is then instructed to "'square off' the shoulders."

e. The singers are finally requested to "hold the head high" and to "move it freely from side to side and up and down."

In standing the following suggestions apply:

a. The singers are told to "direct the weight firmly toward the feet."

b. They are reminded that "the feet should be slightly apart with the toes turned out to a certain extent and with one foot a little in advance of the other."

c. They are instructed to "keep the body straight with no flabbiness at knees or hips."

d. They are admonished, as when sitting, to "'square off' the shoulders," and to "stand to the greatest possible height."

e. They are directed to "hold the head high" and "move it freely in all directions.."

f. They are asked to "drop the arms loosely to the sides" or "clasp the hands lightly at a point just above the waistline."

An exercise for developing proper tension may begin with the request that the students assume the standing posture indicated above. The singers are then instructed to move the body to the right and to the left with all the movement coming from the ankles. If the muscular structure is properly flexed, the students can sway from side to side without losing balance. It is suggested that the sensation is something like that of a tree swaying in the wind. If the bodily structure is too relaxed, the students will lose balance and waver uncertainly; if the bodies are too taut, sidewise motion will be impossible. Having attained some proficiency in maintaining a sense of balance which permits easy motion from side to side, the students are next requested to sway from front to back in the same fashion, that is, without changing the position of the feet, all of the motion coming from the ankles. It is essential in this type of exercise that the feet be placed slightly apart. The base of support must be neither too narrow nor too wide, but so spaced that the body is balanced easily and comfortable.

The director must emphasize that the singers are expected as a matter of course to assume the proper physical attitude whenever they prepare to sing. As soon as the group understands this point, attention should be given to the development of breath control. As with all problems in singing, the need for work along this line can best be demonstrated through the use of actual music. The director should select for rehearsal some composition which is calculated to demand rather more breath than can be easily supplied. When, in the course of the singing, the student realizes that his breath supply is inadequate, he is forcibly made aware of the necessity for extending his power and thereby may become receptive to concentrated drill. At that point the following procedures may be found effective.

The singer is requested to stand, assuming the position discussed earlier. He is instructed to locate the floating ribs, placing the index fingers directly under them and stretching the thumbs backward toward the backbone as far as possible, at the same time stretching the tips of the fingers as far forward as he is able. Holding the chest and shoulders high, he is instructed to exhaust the lungs. Often violent physical activity can be noted, usually involving excessive collapse of chest and shoulders. The singer must learn that exhaustion of breath is to take place without visible movement in this region. As he expels the breath, he is told to maintain the chest and shoulders "high and quiet." In this way attention is directed to the activity which necessarily must take place at the diaphragm. The singer is told that as he expels his breath the waistline should contract and the tips of the index fingers approach each other. He is then instructed to inhale, and as he does so to note that the tips of the index fingers are pushed apart. All of this is to be accomplished with a minimum of visible physical activity.

The group may now be instructed to exhale and inhale in rhythm, with hands on waists as directed. Most of the expansion will be felt in the fingertips, but some should be felt also in the fleshy part of the hand along the base of the thumb, and, although to a lesser degree, even in the thumbs themselves.

The singer is now requested to sit or stand "to the greatest height." If the natural chest position is a normally high and active one, no further comment need be made in this connection. If, however, the individual shows a tendency to slump, he may be told to assume a chest position which would suggest vital physical activity. He is instructed to place one hand on the chest and to blow the breath from the lungs. If excessive motion occurs, he is requested to repeat the procedure, watching to see that the hand remains quiet on the chest. He is likewise told to inhale, again keeping the hand stationary on the chest, with all of the activity taking place at the waist. At this point the singer is requested to open the palm of the hand and to place the open hand in the general region of the waistline, where the result of diaphragmatic action may be felt during a process such as that outlined above. He is instructed to note that when the chest is high and quiet the process of inhalation produces a muscular expansion at the diaphragm, apparent in the outward movement of the hand. Conversely, as breath is exhaled without visible chest activity the hand comes inward with a contraction of the diaphragmatic muscles.

The student is now requested to place one hand on the chest and the other at the diaphragm. When this procedure is applied in group work, the students may be instructed to inhale and exhale in rhythm, keeping the hand which is placed on the chest quiet during the process and noting the movement of the hand which is placed in the region of the diaphragmatic muscles.

These exercises provide an indirect method for securing proper support without even a mention of the term "diaphragm." Whether or not the instructor wishes to go into technical vocabulary and detailed analysis of procedures depends on his own views regarding educational techniques and upon his skill in developing technical knowledge without a resultant loss of interest in music as an activity. If he so desires, the director may indicate that the type of breath control discussed above is known as "diaphragmatic-intercostal" breathing. This term has reference to a control effected by the interaction of the diaphragm and the intercostal, or rib, muscles. While the diaphragm itself cannot be felt, the result of the interaction of diaphragmatic and intercostal muscles is observable in the expansion and contraction of the waistline discussed above.

Let it be emphasized that the activity taking place must arise from actual movement of the breath, not as a mere expansion and contraction of the muscular apparatus. It is possible to produce expansion and contraction through mechanical action of the abdominal muscles, having no connection with, or effect upon, breathing. If the physical activity at the waistline does not result from the action of the breath it is of no value. Therefore, it must be employed only as a means to an end, and should not be cultivated for itself alone.

Once the matter of posture and breathing has been thoroughly understood, it is not expected that time in subsequent rehearsals will be devoted to re-analysis of the process. It should be made clear that this is the first singing habit which is to be established as a part of the singing procedure. Thereafter it is to be taken as a matter of course that a proper physical attitude will be assumed for any type of singing, even for performing informally and without direction. Singers are expected to make this as much a part of their activity as a good swimmer or a fine tennis player makes a proper stroke habitual to his performance, no matter when or where he carries on the activity.

Tone quality is closely related to the matter of physical preparation, since the cultivation of good tone is conditioned to a high degree by the physical reaction of the singing mechanism. There are, in addition, other factors bearing upon production, notably that of diction, but at the moment, consideration will be given to the more purely physical aspects of the problem.

First, the mouth should open in a generally vertical direction. Many untrained singers are inclined to open the mouth horizontally, particularly in certain parts of the country. A horizontal opening tends to produce colorless tone, described in common usage as "white." Such a tone lacks roundness and depth as a general rule, and is usually uninteresting. Instructing the singers to open their mouths vertically usually will bring a more positive character into the tone. The group must learn to think of the lips as an active physical organism. The lips of many beginning singers are flabby and immobile, lacking in physical energy. The idea of *shape* in the mouth formation should constantly be held before the singer. The student should think of the lips as an actively moving mechanism, possessing a certain characteristic conformation and operating with precision and accuracy. The tip of the tongue should receive careful attention. The singer should think of it as thin and pointed, and as working, in general, against the lower teeth. In order to bring the tone into proper focus and to secure definition in projection, the tongue tip must be accurate in its action. Lack of positiveness in this respect leads to tone that is wanting in point, a type of tone that may be characterized as "mushy." The tongue should rest in the mouth in a generally flat position. Attention should also be directed toward the middle and back of the tongue. As in other parts of the singing mechanism, the muscles here are often flabby. Consequently the tongue is over-relaxed and occupies too much space in the mouth. Thus part of the resonating cavity is shut off, and the tone loses brilliance, sounding thick and muffled.

The concept to be desired is that of the tongue resting flat in the mouth with a small channel in its center. The tongue should be depressed and kept out of the way so that resonance is not obstructed. The singer can note this depression by placing one finger on the tongue. His finger should lie in the groove without gagging him or causing discomfort. If, in the application of this procedure, these tendencies are apparent, it follows that the tongue is too high in the mouth. The director will need to apply the procedure with humor and skill, but he can employ it with great effectiveness in demonstrating to the singer the need for vitality and crispness in tongue activity.

To recapitulate, the singer must think of the tongue as an active muscular apparatus, moving quickly and precisely, lying low in the mouth, depressed in the center, with the tip moving freely and lightly against the lower teeth. These procedures will help greatly to clear up tone that is "clothy" and dull, and serve especially in preparing passages in which rapidity and lightness are desired.

The position of the jaw is most important in securing good quality. The movement of the jaw should be free and relaxed, and at the same time resilient. The jaw should be free from tension and any feeling of being held at the back, yet it should not be allowed to hang loosely. The singer may be told to think of the jaw as operating on a hinge, unimpeded yet supported. Any suggestion of wobbling or of shaking in the movement of the jaw should be avoided. Such movement alters the formation of the resonating cavity and causes the tone to fluctuate in quality. Variation in pitch also is likely to result from the constantly changing shape of the singing mechanism.

A frequent deterrent to good quality is the fact that inexperienced singers often allow themselves to shut off the upper part of the resonating cavities. The tone may seem flat in contour because there is not enough breath pressure to send the tone into the upper part of the resonator. The resulting sound may seem to be lifeless or pallid and lacking in vigor. Often the lack of resonance is due to insufficient physical exertion. Energizing of the physical attitude is frequently effective as a corrective. A stronger impulse should be produced with the diaphragm, and more energy directed toward supplying the breath in a steady stream from the diaphragm to the resonator.

Lack of character in the tone quality of many singers can be corrected by an idea of "arching" the tone. The thought of "arching," or lifting the tone into the upper part of the resonator, will sometimes bring into the tone the color and animation so urgently desired.

Additional resonance often can be brought into the tone by giving the singer an idea of "focus in the mask." To locate the "mask," the singer is instructed to place the thumb of the right hand on the upper cheek bone, immediately under the right eye, the fourth finger similarly under the other eye with the index finger on the forehead. The triangle thus formed is called the mask. The singer is told to direct the tone into this triangular area. When the upper resonating cavities are brought into play, there can be noted a slight vibration in the bony structure where the fingers rest.

Some singers hamper their tone production by impeding the flow of breath at the throat. Visible evidence of this obstruction appears in distention of the tendons at the back and the sides of the neck. Starting at the diaphragm, the breath should continue upward in a steady, uninterrupted column. The throat muscles must be freed from any constriction that may interfere with this flow. The singer is requested to take the vowel *oh* or *ah* on any given comfortable pitch. He is told to maintain the vowel sound steadily and without any wavering in the tone. As he holds the tone, he is instructed to move his head freely from side to side, and up and down. When he moves his head, it is possible that there will be considerable vibration and variation in the tone level. He is told to eliminate this as much as possible by sending the breath from the diaphragm directly *through* the throat into the resonating cavities. As the singer rotates his head, he is instructed to massage the muscles at the back of the neck, until they are pliant and flexible, and all trace of constraint is removed. It is sometimes helpful to think of the interior of the mouth and the upper resonator as though the structure represented a bandshell. The tone follows along the wall of the shell, reaching a point at the upper and outer edge where it comes downward in an arc to a point of focus in the mask, before dispersing itself to the listener.

CHAPTER III

DICTION: VOWELS

Diction[1], as a matter for consideration by the singer, embraces:

a. *Correct Pronunciation,* involving manner of utterance with regard to sound and accent.
b. *Clear Enunciation,* dealing with clarity and distinctness of delivery.[2]

Pronunciation concerns itself first of all with the correct sounding of the individual syllable, which depends to a large degree on the treatment accorded the vowel. Pronunciation secondly involves the relative weight accorded the various syllables, or, in other words, the problem of proper syllabic accent.

In embarking upon a procedure designed to develop good diction, the approach should be made through the spoken word. The aim is that of speech which is cosmopolitan in character, the speech of an educated person, marked neither by provincialism nor by over-sophistication. The young singer should proceed from the best local speech of his own region, refined and dignified, yet retaining its quality of natural utterance. It should be untinged by incorrect localisms or unnatural mannerisms but should never reach such a point of refinement that it becomes stilted or affected. Artificiality is as great a defect as provincialism.

In dealing with the word, either in speaking or in singing, one must be aware of its two constituents: vowel and consonant. The singer who expects to achieve any degree of proficiency must respect both of these elements. The beauty

---

1 For the purposes of this work, diction will be considered as it relates to the oral treatment of the English language in the United States.

2 In other words, we use the term "diction," in one of its American senses rather than in its original English sense (which has to do with the selection of words, rather than with the manner in which they are sounded).

17

of the diction in large measure depends upon the quality of the vowel. Its clarity results chiefly from the proper articulation of the consonant. Beautiful vowel sounds without clearly articulated consonants result in formlessness. Cleanly articulated consonants without accompanying roundness and purity in vowel formation produce brittleness. The consonant gives spine to the tone; the vowel gives it flesh. Neither element should be developed at the expense of the other.

The skillful treatment of the two components must proceed as a part of the process of synthesis. Neither can be separated from the other in competent singing, nor should they be divided in the course of training. All too often, teachers of singing and choral directors alike give evidence of over-preoccupation with vowel formation. The result of this absorption is a neglect of the problem of clarity in consonantal enunciation. The sung word has little purpose beyond that of making clear the beauty and meaning of the text, intensifying and pointing up its basic implications. Otherwise, nonsense syllables would suffice. The person who confines his consideration of the vocal problem to the cultivation of purely beautiful tone would do as well to relinquish words altogether and to confine himself to wordless syllables. W. J. Henderson, the late American music critic, spoke well to this point when he said, "Singing is the interpretation of text by means of musical tones produced by the human voice. . . . To sing mere sounds is a senseless performance . . . . Let it be understood that in song, as in the Wagnerian drama, the music is not the end, but a means."[3]

Over-concentration upon quality *per se* can easily result in the production of a type of tone that may be beautiful as far as its purely sensuous aspect is concerned but which, at the same time, may be utterly lacking in character. On the other hand, excessive concentration upon projection of the consonant can result with equally bad effect in tone that

3 *The Art of the Singer*, New York, Charles Scribner's Sons, 1906, pp. 5, 6, 8.

may be vital and clear but lacking in requisite physical beauty. Furthermore, over-concentration upon the consonant can easily destroy the fundamental quality of line that is essential to all good music, vocal or instrumental.

Repertoire should be so chosen that the text offers opportunity for the development of tone. Having decided upon an appropriate composition, the director should first present it to the group purely as a work of art, without any comment regarding its possible use for the study of any particular problem. The singers should be given an opportunity to sing the work, or a section of it, as a complete unity. After they have gained some feeling for the composition as a whole, the director may isolate for study those passages that demand greater proficiency in production. Exercises may be improvised from the musical material of the work at hand, or the director may introduce a standard vocalise designed to correct the fault in question.

There is available a wealth of published material containing vocalises intended for the development of tone. Most of these exercises utilize basic vowel sounds in patterns derived from scale material or chord figures. If an approach is to be made through the use of such abstract drill material, this material should be so chosen that the basic problem can be applied immediately to the music under rehearsal. The director must lead the student to realize that proficiency in abstract drill is not to be regarded as a goal in itself, but rather as a means for the improvement of the performance of the literature.

In approaching the development of tone quality in a group with limited previous experience, first attention should be given to the so-called primary vowels, *ee, ay, ah, oh*, and *oo*. Groups vary widely in the treatment accorded these sounds. Some groups will exhibit a notable weakness in singing one or two particular s o u n d s; other groups will handle these in a satisfactory manner but will experience difficulty with other members of the sequence. In some parts of the country there is a characteristically unpleasant pronunciation of certain vowels, while in other localities an entirely different set may be calling for attention. There is no need for the director to linger over sounds that are well sung. On the other hand, he should be alert to note those which are particularly lacking in beauty and should apply concentrated study toward their improvement.

The five-tone descending scale, *sol, fa, mi, re, do,* in quarter-note values upon the vowel sequence, *ee, ay, ah, oh, oo,* may serve as a preliminary exercise in attacking the problem. It may be sung without the piano or with harmonization to provide musical interest. Such an exercise should ordinarily start near second-space *a,* doubled at the lower octave which is a comfortable pitch for the average choral group. It should be extended upward and then downward by half-steps. The young singer should strive to develop an aural consciousness of the vowel sound on each degree of the scale as he sings it. Granted that no singer can ever obtain a complete aural image of his tone exactly as it sounds to the listener, nevertheless he can direct his listening so that he obtains at least something of an impression of his own vocal quality.

If the singers produce an incorrect sound, the director may request the group to pronounce such words as, for example, the following:

a. For the vowel *ee, me.*
b. For the vowel *ay, say.*
c. For the vowel *ah, arm.*
d. For the vowel *oh, so.*
e. For the vowel *oo, moon.*

The group is requested to utter the given word in a speaking voice. There undoubtedly will be variations in the quality of the vowel as pronounced by the group. The singers are directed to repeat the pronunciation, listening intently to the quality of the sound. On successive repetitions, the group is instructed to bring the vowel sound into a "uniform mold"— a consistent quality throughout the group. This will usually bring an improvement in the pronunciation. If it does not do so, the instructor may then stop and repeat the word, first as the group has mispronounced it and then as it would be pronounced correctly. This procedure of direct imitation should be introduced only as a last resort, after other methods have failed.

Americans tend to emphasize the diphthongal aspect of certain vowels or to give vowels a diphthongal quality which they should not properly possess. In the above type of exercise the pure sound of the vowel, that is, its principal element, should be extended, while any secondary element should receive properly subordinate and inconspicuous treatment. Therefore the student is requested to concentrate his listening toward the maintenance of a sound that will be uniform for the duration of the principal element.

The tendency to extend the diphthongal element is illustrated by the vowel *ay*. With this vowel there is a tendency to pass from a pure *ay* to an *ee* at the end, producing the combination *ay-ee*. The singer must make a definite effort to maintain the *ay* for its full duration, minimizing as much as possible the quality of the concluding *ee*. A similar tendency is encountered in the vowel *oh*. Here, instead of maintaining the *oh* sound for its full duration, the singer frequently allows himself to slip from *oh* into *oo* before completing the sound. The long *u* represents a different type of diphthongal sound. Here it is the second sound, that of the *oo* which stands as the principal element, while the initial vowel, a lightly brushed sound with the character of a short *i*, assumes secondary importance. In this case the first element must be sounded rapidly and lightly without any emphasis, and the second element must be extended.

A difficulty commonly encountered is that of properly connecting two successive vowels. One frequently can detect an improperly interjected *y* or *w*. The improper sounding of the consonant *y* arises from excessive activity in the tongue in proceeding from one vowel to the next; the improper sounding of the *w* results from excessive lip activity.

The remedy in each case is to be found in the elimination of superfluous motion in proceeding from one vowel formation to the next, the two still being joined without a break in the flow of the line. All exercises for the development of vowel formation should be used with the above considerations constantly emphasized during the drill. The principles fundamental to correct vowel treatment may be summed up as follows:

a. The formation for each vowel to be pure in character.
b. The quality of the individual vowel sound to be uniform throughout the ensemble.
c. The principal element of the vowel to be maintained for its full duration without distortion through over-emphasis of the diphthongal element.
d. Each vowel to be joined smoothly to the following vowel without disturbance in the flow of the tonal line.
e. The vowel succession maintained to be that of pure vowel sound without interjection of any consonantal sound between the successive vowels.

If in doubt about some detail of pronunciation, the instructor should not rely upon chance surmise. He should have at hand a good dictionary for consultation at all times. It should be an American dictionary, one compiled with specific reference to the speech habits and the best speech usage of the American people.

The dictionary represents the result of exhaustive research by phoneticians, presented in such form that it may be readily accessible. However, the phonetician makes his study a detailed one, and his analysis of speech produces finer subtleties of differentiation than the young singer requires. The chorister attempting to follow every shade of difference indicated by the expert will become involved in a welter of minutiae which will not aid, but confuse him. For this reason, some classification must be adopted to reduce the large number of sounds represented by the phonetician to a basic set useful for the singer. Such a classification follows:

a

1. as in *tale*. The sound may be accented, as in *today*, or unaccented, as in *duplicate*. Webster indicates a diacritical marking for the sound $\bar{a}$ when it is accented; $\bar{a}$ when unaccented *(tōō-dā', dū-pli-kat)*.[4]

2. as in *fare*. The diacritical marking for the sound is $\hat{a}$ *(fâr)*. For all practical purposes in singing, the sound is the same as that employed in the word *sat*, the diacritical marking for which is $\breve{a}$ *(săt)*. The phonetician makes a distinction between these sounds but, as far as the singer is concerned, their basic quality may be considered identical. The latter sound, $\breve{a}$, may be accented, as in *ransom (răn-sŭm)*, or unaccented, as in *accept (ăk-sĕpt)*. The sound of the vowel *a* in the word *task* should be treated as an identical sound. The diacritical marking is $\dot{a}$ *(tàsk)*. The sound may be accented as in *after (àf-ter)*, or unaccented as in *among (à-mŭng)*.

3. as in *arm* The diacritical marking for this sound is $\ddot{a}$ *(ärm)* The *a* in *was* has the same basic sound as far as performance purposes are concerned. Phoneticians consider this latter sound identical with the *o* in such words as *sob*, the diacritical marking for which is $\breve{o}$ *(sŏb)*. The young singer will do well to treat the sound of the *a* in *arm* and of the *a* as in *was* as the same basic sound.

4. as in *tall*. Phoneticians consider this sound the same sound as the *o* in such words as *morn*, the diacritical marking for which is $\hat{o}$ *(tôl, môrn)*.

5. as in *any*. In words of this type, the *a* has the sound of a *short e*, indicated by the diacritical marking $\breve{e}$ *(ĕn-i)*.

---

4 All diacritical markings are taken from *Webster's New International Dictionary of the English Language*, 2nd ed., unabridged, Springfield, Mass., G. and C. Merriam, 1947; "A Guide to Pronunciation" by Paul W. Carhart, rewritten by John S. Kenyon, xxii-lxxviii.

e

1. as in *see*. The sound may be accented as in the second syllable of *redeem*, or unaccented as in the first syllable of the same word. The diacritical marking for the accented sound is *ē* and for the unaccented sound *ė* (*rė-dēm*).

2. as in *set*. The sound may be accented as in *attest*, or unaccented as in *purest*. The diacritical marking for the sound is *ĕ* (*ă-tĕst, pūr-ĕst*).

3. as in *her*. The sound is equivalent to the *u* in *turn* and is represented by the diacritical marking *û* (*hûr*). The sound may be accented, as in *infer* (*in-fûr*), or unaccented, as in *singer*, The final -*er* combination in words such as the latter carries the diacritical marking of -*ẽr* (*sĭng-ẽr*).

4. as in *there*. The sound is equivalent to that of the *a* in *fare*. The diacritical marking for the sound is *â* (*thâr*).

i

1. as in *find*. The diacritical marking is *ī*. It may be accented as in *decide* (*dē-sīd*) or unaccented as in *ideal* (*ī-dē-ăl*). The sound is diphthongal in character, the first element being approximately *ah*, as in *harm*, and the second approximately that of the short *i*, as in *it*. Phoneticians have been unable to describe satisfactorily for the singer the exact sound which the long *i* (*ī*) demands for its proper treatment. In the first element there is something not exactly like any of the sounds indicated for the various pronunciations of the *a* vowel. The formation of this sound may be observed by asking the singers to pronounce some word involving the long *i*, the word *sigh* for example. The singers are requested to extend the vowel sound, bringing it into a uniform mold. It will be remarked that, while the sound possesses a quality which closely resembles that of an *ah* (*ä*), still

there is a slight variation from the *ah* sound which imparts to the long *i* a characteristic color of its own. The second element of the vowel, the short *i*, must be sounded quickly and lightly upon the conclusion of the first element and immediately before proceeding to the next sound.

2. as in *it*. The diacritical marking for the sound is *ĭ*. The sound may be accented, as in the second syllable of the word *fruition (frōo-ish-ŭn)*, or unaccented, as in the word *famine (făm-in)*.

3. as in *stir*. The sound is equivalent to that of the *e* in *her* or of the *u* in *turn*, the diacritical marking for which is *û (hûr, tûrn, stûr)*.

4. as a consonant. When the letter *i* is followed by another vowel, it usually assumes the character of the consonant *y*. For example, the last syllable of the word *alleluia* is customarily pronounced *yah*, and the second syllable of the word *pinion* is pronounced *yun*. (In the case of the word *alleluia*, the pronunciation *ah-lay-loo-ee-ah* is rather special and should be employed only when the rhythmic pattern clearly indicates the need to sound the *i* as a separate syllable).

o

1. as in *so*. The sound may be accented, as in *holy*, or unaccented, as in *oblige*. The diacritical marking for the accented sound is *ō (hō-lĭ)* and for the unaccented sound *ō (ȯ-blīg)*.

2. as in *morn* The sound is equivalent to that of the *a* in *tall*, the diacritical marking for which is *ô (tôl, môrn)*. The vowel sound indicated in Webster by the symbol *ŏ*, as in *off (ŏf)*, is, for the purposes of singing, an equivalent sound.

3. as in *sob*. The diacritical marking for the sound is ŏ *(sŏb)*. The sound may be accented, as in *modern (mŏd-́ ĕrn)* or unaccented as in *observe (ŏb-zûrv́)*.

4. as in *move*. The diacritical marking for the sound is o̅o̅ *(mo̅o̅v)*. The sound is identical to that of *oo* in *soon (so̅o̅n)*.

5. as in the first syllable of the word *bosom*. The diacritical marking for the sound is ŏŏ *(bŏŏź-ŭm)*. The sound is identical to that of *oo* in *book (bŏŏk)*.

6. as in *done*. The sound is identical to that of the *u* in *cup*, the diacritical marking for which is ŭ *(kŭp, dŭn)*. For singing purposes the *o* in *word* proceeds from the same basic vowel sound. These are both equivalent to the sound of the *u* in *turn*, the diacritical marking for which is û *(tûrn, wûrd)*. The sound of the *o* in the suffixes *tion* and *or*, as in the words *creation* and *director*, employs the same basic vowel sound. These sounds are represented by the diacritical markings ŭ and ĕr *(krĕ-á-shŭn, ̌li-rĕk-tĕr)*.

u

1. as in *muse*. The sound may be accented, as in the word *union*, or unaccented, as in the word *unite*. The diacritical marking for the sound is ū when the sound is accented and u̇ when unaccented *(ūn-yŭn, u̇-nīt)*. The sound is diphthongal in character. The principal element is the second, which is in effect that of the *oo* in *soon*. The first element is a sound derived basically from that of the short *i (ĭ)* with something of the quality of the long *e (ē)* added. For example, the word *muse* is properly pronounced neither *mĭ-o̅o̅ź* nor *mē-o̅o̅ź*, but somewhere between the two, rather closer to long *e* than short *i*, for purposes of singing. The essential element in the diph-

thong is the final one, *oo*, with the first element brushed over quickly.

2. as in *rule*. The sound is equivalent to that of the *oo* in *soon*. The diacritical marking for the sound is ōō *(rōōl)*.

3. as in *full*. The sound is equivalent to that of the *oo* in *book*. The diacritical marking for the sound is ŏŏ *(bŏŏk, fŏŏl)*.

4. as in *cup*. The diacritical marking for the sound is ŭ *(kŭp)*. For purposes of singing, the sound is equivalent to that of the *u* in turn, indicated by the diacritical marking û *(tûrn)*, to the *e* in *her*, indicated by the diacritical marking û *(hûr)*, to the *e* in *singer*, indicated ēr *(sing-ēr)*, and to the *i* in *stir*, indicated û *(stûr)*. The sound may be accented as in *thunder (thŭn-dēr)* or unaccented as in *stirrup (stir-ŭp)*.

5. as a consonant. The letter *u* is often encountered in a situation where it is equivalent to *w*. In such cases it is found in combination with *g*, *q*, or *s*, as in *guava, queen, dissuade (qwä-va, kwēn, di-swād)*.

●

It may be observed from the preceding that, for the singer's purposes, the English language employs thirteen basic vowel sounds, grouped as follows:

1. ā, ā
2. â, ă, a
3. ä, ŏ
4. ē, ē
5. ĕ
6. ī
7. i
8. ō, ō
9. ô

10. $\overline{oo}$
11. $\breve{oo}$
12. $\bar{u}, \ddot{u}$
13. $\hat{u}, \breve{u}, \hat{e}$

This classification does not attempt to represent all of the vowel sounds that are possible in English, nor does it make any effort to cope with foreign-language v o w e l s. Rather, it p r e s e n t s a simplified classification of vowel sounds that are basic in the singing of English by the American performer. The singer who has developed his power of directed concentration to the point where he is aware of the fundamental qualities of these classifications and who knows as he sings which of these classifications is proper for the text of the moment will have acquired considerable knowledge of good singing diction.

Admittedly, the young singer cannot be expected to know all these classifications at the outset, and it cannot be assumed that, with the average choral group, the individual members always will be able to classify all the sounds they are employing. That knowledge and that ability, nevertheless, can be acquired, and steady growth in this respect should result from the singing experience of every performer. Thorough knowledge of vowel sounds and basic formations, however, is indispensable for the choral conductor. He must know what the proper sounds are, be able to detect variations therefrom, and know how to set about securing the proper sound. Familiarity with the above classifications will be of aid in this direction.

CHAPTER IV

DICTION: CONSONANTS

It has been pointed out that the audibility and beauty of the tone in large measure depend upon the proper treatment of the vowel, provided that adequate breath support is supplied. The intelligibility for the most part results from proper treatment of the consonant. As in studying vowels, the singer may employ a classification based on, but simplified from, the findings of phoneticians. The processes which result in clear, well-defined speech have to do with the proper articulation of the singing mechanism previously discussed in connection with the movement of tongue, lips, and jaw (pages 13-14).

For purposes of singing, consonants may be classified with regard to the type of articulation needed to bring about their proper enunciation. This is to say that the singer may best accomplish his aim by directing attention to the point of articulation for each consonant. The basic classifications are provided below.

Dentals
d, t, n, l, th

The dental consonants are those which are articulated when the tip of the tongue is brought into contact with the teeth. This is an extremely important family since, first of all, it represents a type of consonant which is frequent in its appearance in the language, and, secondly, it demands a type of utterance in which Americans, as a nation, are notably lax.

In order that the dental consonants may be sounded clearly and distinctly, the tongue must move with alacrity and precision. It must be firm in its movement, with the tip thin and pointed. One of the greatest deterrents to good diction in the United States is the fact that most Americans allow the tongue to become over-relaxed and flabby, moving

29

heavily and thickly in the mouth. In addition, there is a tendency to let the tip of the tongue move weakly and without sufficient quality of point. Both of these difficulties must be overcome if the singer is to achieve even reasonably good singing diction, which is, after all, nothing but a translation into musical tone of good speaking diction.

The conductor will do well, in approaching the study of consonants with young singers, to give first attention to the dentals, keeping before himself and the student the idea that this particular family of consonants requires *(a)* a sensation of firmness and mobility of the tongue as a whole, and *(b)* a sensation of point and decisiveness in the tip. Presentation of the proper treatment for this type of consonant may be made in the following manner. Take, for example, the letter *t*, one of the most important members of the family. In the course of rehearsing some particular selection, the director will be able to note a word or a series of words involving the letter. For instance, in the second chorus of the Brahms *Requiem*,[5] there occurs the phrase, *so be ye patient*. Because of the position of the phrase, at the conclusion of a section, succeeded by an extended rest in the voices, lack of clarity in the enunciation of the final *t* is often obvious. The *t* in question should be sharply enunciated at the point in the measure where it is indicated, that is, at the beginning of the following beat. Most choruses upon first singing the passage will allow the word to fade away in a more or less indiscriminate fashion, possibly without any intimation of the final consonantal sound. Where the director notes such lack of clarity in the enunciation of the final word, he should halt the chorus and call attention to the fact that:

a. The final sound in the phrase is that of the consonant *t*.
b. The sound of the *t* as indicated should come at the beginning of the second beat of the measure.
c. In order for the word to be properly sung, the final vowel

---

5 Reference is made to the English translation appearing in the G. Schirmer edition, p. 17.

sound, in this case a short *e (ĕ)*, should be sustained as long as possible and the *t* sounded clearly and distinctly at the beginning of the following beat.

d. In order for the consonant to emerge as a sharp, clear sound, it is necessary for the tip of the tongue to move with alacrity to the teeth.

At this juncture, the director may indicate that the various consonantal sounds of the English language are classified into certain groups for convenience in singing. He may indicate that *t* is regarded as a dental consonant, and should define the term *dental* at this time. If he chooses, he may introduce the other members of the group at this moment or delay their introduction until they occur similarly, as problem sounds, in the course of subsequent rehearsals. The latter alternative would be preferable in the light of current educational theory.

An attitude of mind can be developed within the chorus whereby the singers become aware of the dental consonants as a problem group and of the consonant *t,* for instance, in particular. They can anticipate the problem involved and appreciate the steps necessary to achieve proper enunciation. It is a great time-saver for the director to be able to say in connection with a certain passage, "Watch for the dental consonants," rather than to stop and rehearse at every point where the sounds in question are being improperly treated. As in the case of the *t,* all the sounds in the dental group require for proper enunciation a sharp, forward movement of the tongue tip toward the teeth.

The degree of difficulty in enunciating any consonant clearly is affected by the position it occupies within the word. A consonant is said to be initial when it occurs at the beginning of a word, intermediate when it appears within the word, and final when it occurs at the end. It is as initials or as finals that consonants, for the most part, offer trouble. They customarily present little difficulty in the intermediate position. Even as an initial consonant a dental does not ordinarily occasion as much difficulty as in the final position though, in some instances, it may be well to request the singers to give more attention to sharpness and precision of utterance. The dental as a final presents a greater problem. The average singer is accustomed to allow the final dental to disappear in what seems to be only an approximation of its true value, as in the example just given.

The following words illustrate the position of the various dentals as initial and final consonants respectively:

a. *d*, as in *do, sad.*
b. *t*, as in *to, sat.*
c. *n*, as in *no, sin.*
d. *l*, as in *low, toll.* This consonant presents rather more difficulty than *d, t,* and *n.* Some authorities designate this consonant a lingual although others classify it as a pure dental. In any event, it is in something of a class of its own and demands somewhat special attention. The term *lingual* implies that the tongue is particularly active in the articulation of the sound. The tongue must move upward with more definition of movement, or more pressure, than is required for clean articulation of the *d, t,* or *n,* in a motion which concludes with a slight flip at a point on the hard palate just back of the upper teeth. As heretofore, the tongue must be firm and flexed, with a sensation of pointedness at the tip. There is to be noted a certain sensation, indicated by the term "lingual roll," applied by some authorities to this consonant. The term may be helpful in giving the chorus an idea of the motion involved.

e. *th.* This letter combination offers a specific problem because it represents two possible sounds:

1. The combination is said to be voiceless, or unvoiced, when it occurs as in the word *thin.* It may appear as an initial, as in the word *thin,* or a final,

as in the word *hath*. The phonetic sign for the voiceless sound consists simply of the letters without any additional marking, thus: *th*.

2. The combination is said to be voiced when it occurs as in the word *there*, where it appears as an initial and in the word *smooth*, where it occurs as a final. The diacritical marking for the voiced sound is that of a horizontal stroke through the combination, thus *th* (*thâr, smo͞oth*), as compared with *thin, hăth*).

Considerable carelessness is often evident in the singing of the voiced sound, particularly when occurring as a final. An example of this particular error may be noted in the customary pronunciation of the preposition *with*, in which the concluding sound is made voiceless, producing a quality of indefiniteness. Firm pressure of tongue against upper teeth is necessary to give proper definition.

Labials
b, p, m, w

Having obtained a certain degree of skill in the execution of the dental consonants, the group will do well to take up next the labials, *b, p, m* and *w*. As the term indicates, these are the lip consonants and must be formed with firm lip pressure.

A special class of sounds known as plosives includes the labials *b* and *p*. The term indicates the characteristically explosive quality necessary for proper enunciation. The plosives require particularly firm labial pressure, which produces a popping sensation at the lips.

The following may be noted as examples of the labial consonants, initial and final:

a. *b*, as in *be, sob*.

b.　*p*, as in *pine, up.*

c.　*m*, as in *me, seem.*

In initial position these sounds do not ordinarily present any great difficulty, although at times it may be necessary to call for greater precision in their utterance. As finals the labials are customarily treated with indifference, and often disappear altogether. The student should exercise great care to see that final labials are sounded clearly and decisively.

d.　*w*, as in *win.* This consonant is chiefly important as an initial. When appearing as a final, as in *row*, it is frequently silent, having little or no phonetic value. In certain words, *how*, for example, the *w* represents the second element of the diphthong *ou*, which letter combination is employed for the phonetic symbol: *hou.* In singing this diphthong, care should be exercised to avoid over-extension of the *u.* As an initial sound, *w* is closely related to the vowel sounds of $\overline{oo}$ and $\breve{oo}$. In this position, it is often allowed to take on an excess of the vowel quality. The word *were*, for instance, is often allowed to sound $\overline{oo}$-*ûŕ*, rather than, as it properly should, *wûr.* The difficulty arises when the lips, instead of forming the initial *w* with a firm, distinct and instantaneous movement, operate flabbily and loosely, giving a quality of haziness to the sound. The singer should proceed through the initial consonant without over-extending it and reach the vowel immediately. The lips should come together firmly to form the initial *w* and should open promptly to allow for the formation of the following vowel sound.

Labio-dentals
f, v

The labio-dentals involve action of the lower lips against the upper teeth. They may occur as initials, or finals. In the initial position they do not usually present any considerable problem. As finals they are customarily slighted, or, in some instances, ignored altogether. Close concentration should be directed toward recognizing them as finals, and care should be exercised to articulate them distinctly. In order that they may issue with vitality and precision, the lower lip must move quickly and decisively to the upper teeth at the exact moment that they are sounded. The action should be instantaneous and should not be allowed to prolong itself unduly. The following examples are to be noted:

a. *f.* There are two sounds which are possible for this consonant:

1. The sound may be voiceless, as in the word *feel.* In this instance, it appears as an initial. The voiceless sound may also be employed as a final, as in the word *off.* The term *soft f* is sometimes used to indicate the voiceless treatment of the sound.

2. The sound may be voiced, as in the word *of.* It is a sound equivalent to that of *v.* The term *hard f* is sometimes applied to the voiced sound. The voiced *f* appears only as a final, never as an initial.

b. *v.* The sound is a voiced one in English, the voiceless *v* not properly appearing in that language. Accordingly, it is essential that the voiced *v* be sounded firmly and decisively without any suggestion of the voiceless character of the soft *f.* The presence of the latter quality suggests dialect and should be carefully eliminated from the singing of non-dialectal literature. It imparts a comedic effect out of keeping with the performance of art music. The *v* may appear initially, as in the word *vain,* or as a final, as in the word *move.* In the latter word, the final *e* is silent and without phonetic value, so that the final sound is in reality that of the *v*.

The letter combinations *ph* and *gh* often occur as voiceless labio-dentals, as in the words *phone, seraph, cough*. Their treatment is then identical to that accorded the soft *f*.

Sibilants
s, soft c, z, soft g, j

The group of consonants known as sibilants represents one of the most troublesome sound types in the English language, the obstacles to proper treatment being peculiarly difficult to surmount.

The principles prerequisite to proper treatment of the group are as follows:

a. The sound should be of minimum duration. Prolongation results in an unpleasant hissing quality. Being purely consonantal in character and possessing no vowel quality of its own, a protracted hissing sound completely destroys all semblance of vocal line. There is no greater enemy to beauty of tonal line as such than the over-prominent sibilant. The only exception to this principle of minimum duration occurs when a sibilant may be emphasized or extended for certain descriptive or dramatic effects.

b. The enunciation of the sibilant sound must be instantaneous throughout the group if any degree of perfection in ensemble is to be attained. The difficulty encountered by the solo singer in dealing with the sibilant is multiplied many times in choral performance. The moment of articulation must represent a perfect synchronization among all the choristers, and must take place at the exact metrical point indicated by the score. When a final sibilant is succeeded by a rest, it should be articulated exactly on the beat or the fractional part of the beat as indicated. When a sibilant is succeeded immediately by another sound, either consonant or vowel, the moment of sounding the sibilant should occur as late as possible within the syllable. The vowel preceding the sibilant should be sustained as long as possible, and the sibilant should be sounded quickly, immediately before moving to the succeeding sound.

The following are the most readily noted English sibilants:

a. *s.* The consonant has two different possibilities of sound:

1. It is said to be voiceless when it occurs as in the words *sun* and *hiss.* In the former, it appears as initial; in the latter, as final. The sound is occasionally termed "sharp *s.*" The phonetic sign for the sound is provided by the letter *s* *(sŭn, his)*.

2. The consonant is said to be voiced when it occurs as in the word *his.* This sound is occasionally described as "soft *s.*" It is an identical sound to that of *z*, which letter is employed in writing it phonetically *(hiz)*.

b. *c,* as in *face.* This treatment, often known as the "soft c." is voiceless and is identical with the voiceless or sharp *s.* The sound may be initial, as in *cease,* or final, as in *face (sēs, fās)*.

c. *z.* This consonant has two possible sounds:

1. It is voiced, as in *zone, buzz,* and may occur either as initial or as final; it is phonetically written with the letter *z (zon, buz)*.

2. In certain situations it is equivalent to a voiced *sh* and is represented *zh,* as in *azure (ăzh-ẽr)*.

d. *g,* as in *gentle,* may be considered a sibilant as far as the purposes of singing are concerned. This consonant is sometimes known as the "soft g." It may occur initially, as in the word cited above, or as a final, as in the word *edge.* (In the latter word, the concluding *e* has no phonetic value.) The soft *g* is equivalent to *j,* which letter is employed as the phonetic symbol for the sound *(ĕj, jĕn-t'l).*

e. *j,* as in *jet.* The sound is identical to soft *g,* discussed immediately above.

The following letter combinations represent sounds characterized by sibilance:

a. *sh,* as in *shine, hush.*

b. *ch,* as in *cheek, lurch.*

Particular attention should be given to the differentiation between voiceless and voiced sibilants. If the voiced sound is required, care must be exerted to produce it with a securely voiced character. There is a tendency to allow the voiced sibilant to take on too much of the quality of the voiceless sound. Such a flaw in diction not only denotes lack of accuracy in thought, but suggests use of dialect and creates a comic effect where it may not be intended.

To sum up: Sibilants must be treated carefully whether occurring as initials or as finals. However, it is in the position of a concluding sound that faulty diction in this respect is most apparent. The error is due chiefly to the fact that the singer does not maintain the vowel for the full duration proper to it but allows the sibilant to begin to sound too early in the syllable. He should keep before him the idea of stretching the vowel to its fullest possible extent and then sounding the sibilant instantaneously and decisively before proceeding to the next sound.

Palatals
r, y

The consonants *r* and *y* are known as palatals, owing to the fact that, for their proper articulation, the tongue must come to a point of approximation on the hard palate. With *r*, the tip of the tongue is involved. With *y*, the contact is made with the palate and a point just in advance of the middle of the tongue.

a. *r.* This consonant merits strenuous concentration in the first stages of study, first, because of the frequency with which it appears in English, and secondly, because it is one of the most troublesome sounds in the language, particularly from the standpoint of singing usage. No other consonant except a sibilant can so easily destroy vocal style as an improperly treated *r*, which is often produced with an unpleasant grinding, burring quality. The consonant should receive different treatment according to the position it occupies with reference to the vowel sounds preceding and following. The positions in question are as follows:

1. *Initial* as in *row*. In this position the *r* should be strongly trilled. For a proper trill the tongue must be flexible and yet firm in its action. All suggestion of flabbiness or of inertness must be studiously avoided. The tongue tip should flutter lightly on the hard palate, at a point directly back of the upper teeth. The point of contact should be as far forward as possible in order to obtain a proper focus of tone. Allowing the point of approximation for the *r* to slip toward the back of the mouth displaces the focus. The *r* desired is Italianate in character. Above all, in singing English there should be no suggestion of the quality of the Germanic *r*, which is formed in the

back of the mouth. This *r* possesses an essentially guttural quality which, insofar as is possible, should be eliminated from English diction.

2. *Intermediate,* as in *very.* The consonant is said to be in intermediate position when it occurs between two vowels, either within a word, as in *very,* or when, though appearing at the end of a word, it follows one vowel and immediately precedes another which begins a new word, as in *for all.* In the intermediate position, the *r* should be rolled, or half-trilled. As to formation and point of approximation the half-trill is exactly like the full trill. It is, however, of shorter duration. Again, the point of the tongue should flutter lightly on the hard palate, at a point just back of the upper teeth.

3. *Final,* as in *ever.* The consonant is said to be final when it is followed by another consonant or when it, itself, is the concluding sound, that is, when it is not succeeded immediately by a vowel, as in *ever, ever thus, everlasting.* In the final position, the *r* should be minimized, sounded lightly, though not altogether ignored. The omission of final *r* is a fault in diction, just as the burring quality of over-emphasis is a fault. Proper treatment demands a light sounding of the consonant with careful attention to obtaining pure quality in the vowel immediately preceding.

b. *y,* as in *yet.* This consonant generally offers little difficulty. For its clear articulation, the forward part of the tongue must move decisively toward the hard palate, with the tip pressed lightly but firmly against the lower teeth. As a consonant, *y* occurs only as initial. It has no consonantal quality in the final position. As a vowel, *y* is equivalent to the following sounds:

1. $\bar{i}$, as in *rhyme*.
2. $\breve{i}$, as in *rhythm*.
3. $\hat{u}$, as in *myrrh*.

Aspirate
h

The aspirate, or breath consonant, *h*, offers little difficulty when it is not combined with another consonant sound. It occurs as the initial consonant of a word or syllable, having no sound as a final. For example, in a word such as *oh*, the concluding *h* is silent and without phonetic value.

The consonant often appears in combination with *w*, as in *where*. The actual sound of the combination is correctly indicated *hw*, the aspirate quality of the *h* preceding the labial quality of a firmly sounded *w*, Often the aspirate is slighted or disappears altogether in this combination with the result that, the word *when*, for example, sounds incorrectly *wĕn* instead of *hwĕn*.

The combination partakes of the character of the labial as well as of the aspirate, and, for its proper articulation, firmness in the movement of the lips following the emission of breath is an absolute essential.

Gutturals
hard c, hard ch, k, hard g, q, x

In the initial position, the gutturals seldom demand any particular attention. As finals, however, there is a tendency to slight them somewhat. If greater clarity is desired in their articulation, a firm movement of the middle of the tongue to the roof of the mouth will usually produce the proper result.

Following are examples of the English guttural consonants:

a. *c*, as in *case*. The consonant is described as a "hard *c*" in this usage. It is identical in character to *k*, which letter is employed for its phonetic sign *(kās)*.

b. *ch*, as in *chorus*. The combination is also identical with *k*. It may occur initially, as in *chorus*, and also as final, as in *ache (kō-rŭs, āk)*. In the latter word, the concluding *e* is silent, and the final sound is in reality the *ch*.

c. *k*, as in *keep*. The sound may be initial, as in *keep*, or final, as in *back*.

d. *g*, as in *get*. The *g* in this usage is described as a "hard *g*." The sound may be initial, as in *get*, or final, as in *beg*.

e. *q*, as in *quick*. The consonant itself is equivalent to *k*. It occurs in English only in combination with *u*. The combination *qu* is, in effect, usually an equivalent sound to that of *kw*, partaking of the quality of both guttural and labial. For clarity in articulation, it is essential that the lips make a decisive forward movement immediately after the sounding of the guttural *k*. In a few instances, as in the word *quay*, the combination is equivalent to the guttural *k* alone, without any of the quality of the labial *w*.

f. *x*. This consonant has two possible treatments:
   1. It may be voiceless as in *six*, where it is equivalent to *ks*. The second sound is obviously a sibilant and must be treated accordingly.
   2. It may be voiced, as in *exist*. The quality of the voiced *x* may be indicated *gz*. Customarily inaccurate treatment of the voiced *x* allows it to go voiceless. For instance, the word *exist* sounds improperly *ĕk-sĭst,'* more often than correctly, *ĕg-zĭst.'*

   Neither the unvoiced nor the voiced *x* occurs initially in words of purely English origin. In some words of foreign derivation, the letter *x* occupies the initial position, as in *xylophone*, but in such cases it has the sound of *z*, and is

so written phonetically *(zī-lō-fŏn)*. The unvoiced
x appears as a final as in the word *six (siks)*
cited above.

Special Problems

Certain combinations of consonantal sounds present
problems requiring special treatment. Some of these combinations may be cited as follows:

a. *Double consonants.* In the case of double consonants of identical character, the first should be omitted altogether, and the second sounded particularly
clearly. The vowel preceding the first is maintained
for the full duration of the note accorded to the given
word or syllable. For example, in the succession
her rose, the vowel *û*, in *her (hûr)*, is sustained as
long as possible; the first *r* is omitted altogether;
and the second *r* is rolled clearly, the *r* in this instance being an intermediate one. In a succession
such as *with thee*, the *i* of the first word is maintained for the full duration of the value allotted the
word, the first *th* is ignored, and the second is
strongly voiced.

b. *Successive consonants of same group.* In the case
of two consonants belonging to the same family, the
two are merged. In the succession *his sign*, two sibilants appear in succession, the first properly voiced
and the second unvoiced. The first final starts with
the sound of a voiced sibilant, but, in its conclusion, resolves itself into the voiceless sibilant
which is initial in the second word. In a succession
such as that of the words *sad tear*, the sound of the
first final, the dental *d*, is merged into that of the
second initial, the dental *t*. In *love for*, the first final
begins with the voiced labio-dental *v*, but a fusion is
made with the voiceless *f* which begins the second
word.

c. *r following a plosive.* The *r* in this position should be strongly trilled, as in *praise, bright.* There is a customary tendency to leave the *r* untrilled in such a situation, with the result that the focus of tone is thrown backward beyond the point of favorable quality. Following other consonants, the *r* is left untrilled, as in *true, dread, frown, green, crown.* When *r* is preceded by a dental, the focal point of the dental is sufficiently forward to provide optimal quality without trilling the *r.* The same may be said for the combination of *r* with the labio-dental *f.* It is difficult to secure a trilled *r* following a guttural; the approximation points of the two consonants are so widely separated that the excessive tongue motion required is great enough to counteract any helpful result which the trilled *r* would ordinarily produce.

d. *th following a sibilant.* In a sequence of words such as *is thine,* the *th* has a tendency to disappear in a merger of the sibilant into the dental. For clear articulation, the singer will need to give particular attention to forming the *th* with a true dental character. This will demand a definite forward stroke of the tongue tip toward the teeth. In drilling upon this problem, the idea of sending the point of the tongue *through* the teeth will usually secure the decision needed.

e. *A dental followed by long u.* The succession of *t* or *d* followed by the long *u* (*ū*) demands a unique treatment of the dental. Examples appear in the words *nature* and *verdure.* Correct treatment produces a sound lying midway between a pure dental and a light sibilant. For instance, the pronunciation of *nature* should be something like what is indicated by *nā'-chŭr.* The second syllable should not be allowed to take on an excessively sibilant character. Nevertheless, the initial consonant in the second syllable exhibits something of the character of a sibilant, but one which is, so to speak, understated, as against the decidedly heavy overstatement which it receives from many individuals. Overstatement results in the sounding of the combination *tu* as though it had been written *chū*. The word should not sound *nā-chūr*; neither should it sound *nā'-tūr* with the *t* sharply separated from the *u*. Properly the dental must be merged into the vowel. Webster indicates the fusion by a connective line at the base, thus: *nā'-tŭr*.

The combination *du*, as in the word *verdure*, involves the quality of the dental *d* with something of the sibilant *j*. The correct pronunciation consists of a sound lying midway between that indicated *vẽr'-dūr* and that indicated *vẽr'-jūr*. The fusion of the *d* and the *u* is indicated by the connective line in the spelling *vûr-dŭr*.

•

The following tables summarize consonantal classifications:

Dentals: d, t, n, l, th

Labials: b, p, m, w

Labio-dentals: f, v

Sibilants: s, soft c, z, soft g, j, sh, soft ch

Palatals: r, y

Aspirate: h

Gutturals: hard c, hard ch, k, hard g, q, x

•

b: labial (plosive)

c: (1) soft, sibilant

  (2) hard, guttural

d: dental

f: labio-dental

g: (1) soft, sibilant

  (2) hard, guttural

h: aspirate

j: sibilant

k: guttural

l: dental (lingual)

m: labial

n: dental

p: labial (plosive)

q: guttural

r: palatal

s: sibilant

t: dental

v: labio-dental

w: labial

x: guttural

y: palatal

z: sibilant

CHAPTER V

PRONUNCIATION PITFALLS

The term "pronunciation," as an element of diction, has to do with the individual word, referring to *(a)* quality of physical sound, *(b)* relative accent accorded the various syllables. Since the vowel so largely determines physical quality, the singer must be certain of the sound appropriate to each vowel.

He must be aurally aware of each syllable as he sings it. In the early stages, directed concentration will be necessary if the performer is to perceive the quality of the sound he produces. However, by continual directed listening, the ear of the student can become so alert that aural consciousness will become a part of the synthesized activity, one of the elements of the total singing process. As one of the skills involved in singing, it can be developed to the point that it will operate automatically and more or less subconsciously. The young singer obviously cannot be expected to know the correct pronunciation of all of the words in the English language, but with the instructor's aid he should build up a vocabulary of correct pronunciation as he proceeds. Environment, experience, and association may have led him to accept as proper a pronunciation which may be erroneous. It may be that the false pronunciation is due to incorrect production, that the formation being employed by the student renders correct pronunciation impossible. Here it is the mission of the instructor to point out basic errors and the means for their correction. The singer should realize that there are a great number of mispronunciations in daily speech which he must take particular pains to avoid. The daily speech habits of the average person do not, unfortunately, represent the most cultivated treatment of the language. Most mispronunciations are due either to carelessness or to ignorance. The intensification of speech which singing represents makes these mispronunciations more than

47

ordinarily apparent. Some common mispronunciations to be avoided by the singer may be grouped as follows:

A. Vowel sounds

a

1. *à.* In all words involving a syllable consisting of the unaccented *à,* the singer must guard against mispronouncing the vowel as though it were a short *u (uh)* and must make certain to give it its own proper quality. For instance, the word *among* is all too often sung *ŭ-mŭnǵ,* rather than, correctly, *à-mŭnǵ.* In an effort to avoid the unpleasant and incorrect sound of the short *u,* some authorities treat the unaccented *à* as though it were identical to the *a* in *arm (ärm).* Properly, *à* should have enough roundness to lend it dignity, without destroying its naturalness. Substituting the broad *ä* suggests preciosity just as use of the *ŭ* suggests lack of knowledge.

2. *ä.* A customary laxness in the pronunciation of the *ä* allows it to turn toward the sound of the short *u (ŭ)* The words *was* and *what* often sound *wŭz* and *hwŭt* respectively, rather than, as is indicated properly for them, *wŏz* and *hwŏt, ŏ* being equivalent to *ä.*

3. The *a* in the word *any,* which Webster indicates as a sound equivalent to a short *e (ĕ),* is often mispronounced *in-i,* rather than, as it should be sounded, *ĕn-i.*

e

1. *ē.* The singer should be particularly watchful for the long *e* when it occurs in an unaccented syllable. Too often it becomes indiscriminate in character, losing the quality of a pure *ee,* and taking on something of a haziness suggesting a sound midway between a short *i* and a short *u.* For example, the word *delay,* may become incorrectly rather like *di-lā́* or *dŭ-lā́,* instead of the correct

de-la. The initial vowel should retain the quality of a pure *ee*, sounded without stress or accent. Again, unaccented long *e (ē)*, is often converted into short *e (ĕ)* Thus the word *despise (de-spīz)* becomes *dĕ-spīz.* The vowel of the initial syllable should be given the sound of *ee (ē)*, not that of *eh (ĕ)*. In many cases, the incorrect treatment of this particular word and others of similar type arises because too much stress is given the first syllable. The over-accentuation strikes the singer's ear as incorrect, and, in an effort to counteract the over-prominent *ee (ē)*, he turns the vowel toward *eh (ĕ)*, thereby falling between two stools. The appropriate treatment will result from awareness on the singer's part as to the exact quality which is becoming to this sound and at the same time its proper accentuation. The customary mispronunciation of the unaccented long *e* usually is to be remedied by giving it the sound of a pure *ee*, produced lightly, without undue prominence.

2. *ĕ.* The following mispronunciations of unaccented short *e* are often to be noted:

   a. As the *u* in *cup.* For instance, the word *dearest* is often sounded *dēr-ŭst*, rather than, as is proper, *dēr-ĕst.* This effect is all the more unpleasant when the final syllable of the word is over-accented, as often happens.

   b. As the *i* in *it.* For instance, such a word as *endure* is often allowed to sound *in-dūr* rather than *ĕn-dūr*, as it should.

i

1. *i.* In the case of the long *i*, two difficulties are commonly encountered:

   a. The first element is excessively broadened.

b. The second element is distorted. The fact that the long *i* is diphthongal in character and proceeds from a sound based upon *ah (ä)* has caused many vocalists to twist it into an improper contour. The first element, *ah (ä)*, is exaggerated, and the second changed from short *i* to long *e*, the result being a too broad *ah-ee*. Thus the word *light*, frequently becomes *lah-eet*. The extreme of the *ah* quality should be avoided, and the second element should possess the character of a lightly sounded short *i*. The singer must sustain the first element through most of the allotted duration, not allowing the second element to enter prematurely but sounding it quickly and deftly just before moving to the next sound.

2. *ĭ.* When the short *i* occurs in an unaccented position, there is a rather common tendency to give it the sound of *uh (ŭ)*. This is to be avoided. For example, the word *famine* should be pronounced *făm-ín*, not *făm-ŭn*. The word *peril* is to be pronounced *pĕr-íl*, not *pĕr-ŭl*.

o

1. *ŏ.* When the vowel *ŏ* occurs unaccented, it is sometimes uttered as though it were a short *u (ŭ)*. For instance, the word *confirm* is often allowed to sound *kŭn-fûrm*, rather than, properly, *kŏn-fûrm*. The word *observe* becomes *ŭb-zûrv*, rather than, correctly, *ŏb-zûrv*.

2. *o* in such words as *creator, director* etc. A common mispronunciation may occur because the singer has a mistaken idea of the proper pronunciation of this vowel. The conscientious student may naturally presume that the *o* in the last syllable of the word *creator* is to be sung as it appears. Thus he gives it the sound of the long *o* as in *so*, making the word sound *krē-ā-tōr*, or possibly, of the *o* in *for*, producing *krē-ā-tôr*. Phoneticians accept

the sound of $\breve{e}(\hat{er})$ as the proper pronunciation characteristic of American speech, so that the word is properly
sung $kr\breve{e}\text{-}\bar{a}\text{-}t\hat{er}$, as a glance at the dictionary would reveal. The sound of $\hat{e}$ has, for the purposes of the singer,
the quality of the u indicated $\breve{u}$ or $\hat{u}$, as in *turn*. The use
of the o quality in singing such words as *creator, direc-
tor*, constitutes an unnecessary affectation. The natural
short u should be employed, being sung with such roundness and polish that it achieves dignity of utterance
without false sophistication.

u

Long u is the sound of all sounds in American speech
where there is to be observed the greatest divergence in
usage. The following words may be taken for illustration:
muse, tune, lute, blue. In the first three the vowel sound is
diphthongal in character. Consisting of two elements, the
second element, long oo, as in *soon*, is the principal one.
Diversity of treatment arises from the variation in quality
accorded the first of these elements.

The word *muse* is properly said or sung only when the
vowel sound has the quality of long e $(\bar{e})$ as its first element. The $\bar{e}$ should not be over-emphasized or extended. It
should proceed immediately to the principal, second element, but without assuming any guise other than that of an
unaccented long e. In the word *tune*, the vowel should be
treated in identical fashion. The pronunciation that is appropriate for this word may be indicated *tewn* $(t\bar{u}n)$. Often
the word is improperly pronounced $t\overline{oo}n$, but the substitution
of $\overline{oo}$ for *ew* $(\bar{u})$ is altogether incorrect. The difficulty is due
to the fact that the initial element is ignored or given insufficient attention. Again, the initial element should tend
strongly toward the long e $(\bar{e})$. The particular fault, in this
instance, consists either in (a) treating the first element as
though it were a short i $(\breve{\imath})$, or (b) omitting the first element

altogether. In the first case, the initial element is not sounded with sufficient decision to bring out its true quality. In the second instance, the individual proceeds from the initial consonant directly to the second element of the vowel, skipping its first element entirely.

In the word *lute*, some purists will insist that the initial element of the vowel should be long *e* ($\bar{e}$). On the other hand, many authorities consider that the first element here more nearly approximates a short *i* ($\breve{i}$). The latter choice would seem preferable for American singers. The pronunciation *lewt* ($l\bar{u}t$) is an affectation as far as most Americans are concerned. On the other hand, pronouncing the word *lute* as *loot* is also faulty. The affectation of *lewt* and the crudity of *loot* are equally bad. Proper treatment lies between the two, with a short *i* as the first element of the diphthong.

In the word *blue*, the pronunciation *blū*, employed by many singers—with a vowel sound identical to that in *few* —constitutes a false conception of elegance and a misunderstanding of the pronunciation appropriate for the word. In this case, the singer should proceed immediately from the initial consonantal combination to the *oo* sound without any intermediate vowel. The sound proper for the word is not *blĕ-ōo*, nor is it *blĭ-ōo*, but simply and directly *blōo*.

In some instances, the second element of the long *u* is allowed to sound $\bar{o}$ instead of $\overline{oo}$. For instance, the word *pure* is often given the sound of *pyŏr*. Here both elements of the sound have been allowed to leave the channels of proper contour. The correct sound may be indicated *pĕ-ōor*, in which there is a light brushing over of a long *e* as the first element and an immediate transition, without any sense of syllabic separation, to a sustained long *oo* ($\overline{oo}$).

The singer should be particularly alert for all words in which the *u* appears. He should consult an authoritative dictionary as to the pronunciation fitting for the word. He should, insofar as is possible, employ the same pronunciation in his singing. If the best American usage differs from that advocated by the phonetician, let the singer make the variation in the light of his best judgment, not through ignorance or carelessness, but with full awareness of what the purist advocates and what adjustment good usage demands for the singer.

B. Prefixes, Initial Syllables

The prefix and the initial syllable merit special care. Since in many cases these syllables are unaccented, the vowel frequently receives insufficient attention and is produced without due regard for purity of quality. The aural consciousness of the singer should be so well developed that he is aware of the vowel quality of unaccented as well as accented syllables. Particularly to be noted are prefixes and initial syllables involving the unaccented long e ($\bar{e}$), or the unaccented o, discussed on pages 48-51.

C. Suffixes, Final Syllables

Suffixes and other concluding syllables often lack necessary purity of vowel formation for the same reason as do prefixes: being unaccented, they receive inadequate attention. Careless production here often results in a vowel sound which is indefinite and indeterminate in nature. The concluding syllable, though accentually unimportant, should be sung with due regard for purity in vowel formation.

The following suffixes and concluding syllables are worthy of special comment:

1. -en. This concluding syllable presents something of a special problem. The phonetician i n d i c a t e s that in speech the vowel actually disappears, being merged into the final consonant. This merging is indicated by such marking as $h\bar{a}s'n$ for the word *hasten*. However, the intensification of vowel sound demanded by sung speech

makes it imperative to assign the concluding syllable a definite vowel quality. The quality that should be employed is the basic sound from which the merged, or elided, vowel has originated, to wit, the short e *(ĕ)*. In singing the syllable *-en*, the performer must avoid the following mispronounciations:

a. as the *i* in *it*, the word *even* sounding $\bar{e}'\text{-}v\breve{i}n$, rather than, as would be correct, $\bar{e}'\text{-}v\breve{e}n$.

b. as the *u* in *cup*, so that a word such as *hasten* becomes $h\bar{a}\acute{s}\text{-}\breve{u}n$, rather than, properly, $h\bar{a}\acute{s}\text{-}\breve{e}n$.

2. *-er.* In the unaccented combination *er*, two mispronunciations are frequently to be noted. The more obvious of these is that of giving undue prominence to the *r*. The consonant is allowed to sound prematurely and is then over-extended. The consequence is a burring effect which is most unpleasant and which completely destroys the purity of the tonal line. The other common mispronunciation usually grows out of an attempt to counteract the grinding quality of the over-prominent *r*. In an effort to avoid this unpleasantness, singers often produce a vowel sound which resembles an *ah (ä)* rather than, more properly, an *uh (û, ê)*. This affectation is frequently noted in the word *ever,* which is sung as though it were written *ehv-ah.* Proper treatment of the syllable *-er* involves the vowel sound of *uh* with a light sounding of the *r* at its conclusion.

Concentration should be directed toward securing a vowel tone based on the short *u (ŭ, û, ê)*, that quality to be sustained for the full duration indicated, and the *r* to be sounded lightly at the conclusion of the syllable immediately before the singer moves to the next sound.

3. *-est.* See discussion of the short *e*, p. 49.

4. *-ful.* When *ful* occurs as a concluding syllable, the final vowel is usually treated as though it were *ŭ* rather than

the correct ŏŏ. The word *cheerful,* for instance, should be sung *chēr-fŏŏl,* not *chēr-fŭl.*

D. Special Problems

1. *Omission of essential sounds.* There is often a tendency to ignore sounds that are essential to the complete value of the word. The following words may be cited in this connection, the sounds customarily omitted being underlined:

   h̲umble

   wh̲ile

   jewe̲l

   rea̲lly

   thous̲a̲nd

2. *Sounding of silent letters.* The following words contain letters that are silent and have no phonetic value. Any sounding of such letters should be avoided:

   pal̲m, correctly *päm*

   wal̲k, correctly *wôk*

   oft̲en, correctly *ŏf'-ĕn*

3. *Substitution of one vowel for another.* The problem has already been discussed on pp. 48-51. It deserves particular attention in the following words because of their frequency of occurrence in the language and their common mispronunciation:

   of. Instead of giving the word the proper quality of an *o (ŏ),* singers and speakers alike often use the sound of *u (ŭ),* resulting in *uhv (ŭv)* rather than, as would be correct, *ahv (ŏv).*

from. The problem here is identical to that above. The word is often sung improperly *frŭm,* rather than properly *frŏm.*

was. There is a tendency to substitute a short *u* for the *a* so that the word sounds *wuhz (wŭz),* rather than, as would be correct, *wahz (wŏz).*

Joseph. This word, of frequent occurrence in liturgical music, should be sung so that the vowel in the final syllable has the quality of a short *e (ĕ).* The word is often incorrectly sung *jṓ-zŭf,* rather than, properly, *jṓ-zĕf.*

Mary. The word is usually given the colloquial pronunciation *merry.* In art music, it should be given the pronunciation of *mā́-ri* or *mấr-i.* In folk music, the colloquial pronunciation of *mĕr-ĭ* is allowable and, as a matter of fact, preferable.

4. *Placing a consonant between two successive vowels.* Many singers, when dealing with a succession of two vowels, as in *see if, high and, thou art,* have an inclination to interject the consonant *y* or *w* between them— *sḗ-yif, hī́-yȧnd, thoú-wärt.* This is the same problem as the intrusion of consonant sounds between the elements of a diphthong, discussed on p. 21, and must be solved in the same way, namely, by eliminating excessive activity of tongue and lips in moving from one vowel sound to the next.

5. *Anticipation of the final consonant.* The singer must resist the tendency to shorten the vowel and utter the consonant prematurely. Such a procedure stops the tone and interrupts the vocal line. Over-emphasis on clarity of diction may sometimes lead singers toward sounding the final consonants too soon. The result is especially disturbing when the consonant is a sibilant or an *m* or *n.* It is also particularly troublesome when an *r* is involved, as in the first syllable of *early* and all words

ending in *-er*, or when *r* appears in a final consonant combination, as in *earth*.

6. *Linking a final consonant to a following initial.* The concluding consonant of a word should be clearly terminated before the initial sound of the following one is produced except in the situation involving identical or similar consonants, discussed under consonantal combinations, p. 43. Ordinarily linking a final consonant to the succeeding sound should be avoided. The problem is apparent in successions such as:

> *feet of them*
>
> *let us now go*
>
> *let us adore*

7. *Addition of a second syllable to one syllable words.* It may be noted that many singers, particularly in the early stages of training, are prone to add a second syllable to words such as the following:

> *hear*, made to sound *hē-ŭr*, rather than, properly, *hēr*.
>
> *hour*, made to sound *ow'-ŭr*, rather than, properly, *our*.
>
> *fire*, made to sound *fĭ-ŭr*, rather than, properly, *fīr*.
>
> *fir*, made to sound *fŭ-ŭr*, rather than, properly, *fûr*.
>
> *bar*, made to sound *bä-ŭr*, rather than, properly, *bär*.
>
> *more*, made to sound *mō-ŭr*, rather than, properly, *mōr*.
>
> *vale*, made to sound *vā-ŭl*, rather than, properly, *vāl*.

8. *Omission of the second of two final consonants.* When a word concludes in a combination of two consonants, the second is sometimes ignored or at least partly slighted. For instance, in the word *went* the final *t* frequently disappears in a fusion with the *n*. Similarly, in the word *Christ*, the final dental often becomes obscured by the

sibilant. Insisting upon clear articulation of the final consonant will usually secure the desired clarity. It may be necessary to reduce the preceding sound slightly. For instance, in order to bring out the *t*, in the word *Christ*, the singer should be instructed to minimize the sibilant and to give more attention to a sharp, forward projection of the final dental.

9. The word *Israel* belongs to no one of the above groups, but it occurs sufficiently frequently in liturgical music to deserve comment. The word admits two different pronunciations in English. When written as a three-syllable word in an English text, the pronunciation is properly *iz-ra-el*. When written as a two-syllable word in English, the pronunciation is *iz-rel*.

E. Accent

The term "accent" refers to the relative weight accorded the syllables within a word, and in a larger sense to the relative weight accorded words within a phrase. In the first sense, to which discussion will be limited for the moment, accent constitutes an element of pronunciation.

It has been observed several times above that problems of pronunciation are related to the accentual values of particular sounds. Certain characteristic errors in accent stem from misconception as to proper treatment and are basically due to lack of knowledge. Here, again, reference to the dictionary provides a simple remedy. However, by far the greater number of misaccentuations are due to carelessness and a general lack of precision.

Particular consideration should be devoted to words of two syllables, where it is easy to place undue emphasis on the unimportant syllable, as in *before, prepare, despise, endure.* Also, the participal suffix *-ing* often receives too much accentual weight in words such as *crying, singing,* *soaring, praising,* and the suffix `-est` is customarily sung with undue emphasis, as in *purest, fairest.* Pronunciation represents the fusion of vowel sound and accent. A study of the two must proceed together.

A recording machine is invaluable in the study of pronunciation. By the aural process, singers often can quickly make discoveries which they come upon in no other way. One hearing of a reproduction of his singing will often demonstrate to the student errors in his performance when no amount of verbal explanation will convince him. Through listening to recordings of their own performance, students often discover mistakes for themselves without comment from the instructor. As a rule, their power of creative thinking is thereby quickened, and they are led to a more critical and investigative attitude regarding their own work.

Many choral organizations throughout the country now have access to recording equipment. It is an ideal situation where the equipment can always be at hand in the rehearsal room. The director has only to note incorrect pronunciations, immediately record the passage in question and play it back to the group without delay. Usually, the singers discover the fault instantaneously. If recording equipment is available only on occasion, the director from time to time may note passages in which difficulties occur. He can make arrangements ahead of time for a certain period in which he may have access to the machine and may devote that time to recording various passages presenting problems upon which he wishes to concentrate. The recordings can then be used for study in subsequent rehearsals.

Recordings by great artists can be utilized with considerable effectiveness in working with a number of vocal problems. A particularly stimulating procedure is possible when two or more different recordings of the same work are available. The students should be instructed to note differences—and to decide which represents a higher ideal of good singing. Such an approach helps to develop the power of aural consciousness and stimulates critical insight and discrimination.

In concluding the consideration of pronunciation as a special problem, it is to be noted that some of the basic sounds of the language present no appreciable difficulty. The speech habits of the average person are such that these sounds are automatically produced with proper dignity. On the other hand, a number of sounds are usually produced incorrectly and will demand the singer's close attention. Between the two extremes lie sounds of intermediate difficulty, which, while not presenting any great problem, nevertheless merit some degree of caution. The following sounds should be singled out for particular study, since they comprise a group customarily treated incorrectly:

1. In unaccented syllables:

   ȧ, as in *among, about.*

   ê, as in *celestial, believe.*

   ĕ, in the suffix *est*, as in *purest, fairest;* also in the syllable *en*, as in *endure, hasten.*

   ê̆, in the -*er* combination, as in *ever, maker.*

   ĭ, as in *peril, famine.*

   ŏ, as in *confirm, observe.*

   u (o͝o), in the suffix *ful*, as in *cheerful, joyful.*

2. In any position:

   ī, as in *light, irate.*

   ū, as in *endure, music.*

•

With regard to vowel sounds as classified earlier, the following summary may be made of characteristic problems:

1. *ā.* Care should be exercised to see that the sound is sung with purity. This vowel often takes on something

of the quality of the short *e (ĕ)* or veers toward a concluding sound of the long *e (ē)*.

2. *â, ă, ȧ*. The customary difficulty here is flatness of quality in the production. The student must be sure to sing this vowel with roundness and dignity.

3. *ä, ŏ*. Again, it is a matter of imparting to the tone a quality of roundness. Many singers show a tendency to produce with this vowel a tone that is "white" in character.

4. *ē*. This vowel often tends toward a short *i*. Care must be taken that it is sung with a pure *ee* sound.

5. *ĕ*. This vowel often sounds "raw," owing to lack of cover in the formation. The lips should be brought slightly forward, not allowed to stretch across the teeth, and the mouth should assume a generally vertical shape. Improper pronunciations of this sound often result from using short *u* or short *i* incorrectly in place of the short *e*.

6. *ī*. The principal difficulty here is the tendency toward over-extension of the second element of the diphthong, namely, the long *e*.

7. *ĭ*. This sound, as a rule, is one of the least troublesome vowels. It is sometimes sung with insufficient brilliance—a fault which in most cases can be corrected by imparting to the tone something of the character of the long *e*. This should not be overdone, however; the vowel must always retain the character of the short *i* and must not become a long *e* in effect.

8. *ō*. This sound causes comparatively little trouble. In the speech of the average American, it is one of the most nearly satisfactory vowels. It is often of better formation than the vowel sound *ah (ä)* and, for that reason, may be more effective than *ah* in developing good

tone production through its employment in vocalizing exercises. (From the *oh*, transition, of course, should then be made to the other vowel sounds.) Occasionally, however, this vowel is sung in such a fashion that it sounds somewhat colorless. This usually can be corrected by introducing the idea of roundness in production. The lips should be firmly rounded and brought slightly forward, and the sound should be emitted without any distortion of the characteristically long *o* quality.

9. $\hat{o}$. This sound often has the fault of seeming "uncovered." It should be sung with roundness, resonance and a certain sense of covering. Otherwise, it takes on too much of the character of a flatly produced *ah*.

10. $\overline{oo}$. This sound occasionally carries a suggestion of hootiness, which usually can be counteracted by moving the lips with firmness and precision. In case this does not bring the vowel into focus, the idea of narrowing the aperture usually will be of assistance, and, occasionally, the idea of employing a smaller stream of breath will be found effective.

11. $\breve{oo}$. This sound causes comparatively little trouble, although occasionally it takes on too much of the long *oo* quality. Directed listening will usually remove the difficulty.

12. $\bar{u}, \tilde{u}$. The second element of this diphthong, the *oo* sound, is quite commonly exaggerated. Also, some singers mispronounce the initial element. Again it is a matter of knowing the proper pronunciation and of using the ear to detect departures therefrom in either element.

13. $\hat{u}, \breve{u}$. Often this sound takes on too much of the character of *ah* (*ä*). The problem usually arises from *(a)* carelessness in vowel formation, or *(b)* exaggerated avoidance of the succeeding *r*, with which the vowel is fre-

quently combined in English. In the combination of this vowel with *r*, there is a customary tendency to bring in the final consonant too early; in an effort to avoid this pitfall, the singer often goes too far in the other direction and allows himself to produce a highly affected *ah*, with the final consonant completely omitted. The vowel sound should be given its own quality, produced with a sensation of firmness in the lip and mouth formation and with a generally vertical opening of the mouth, the succeeding *r* to be sounded lightly.

The sounds presenting most difficulty and for which the beginning singer should be most alert are:

$\hat{a}$, $\breve{a}$, $\dot{a}$, a sound which, with most beginning singers, either lacks roundness and dignity, or becomes affected and artificial.

$\breve{e}$, which has a tendency toward rawness and lack of roundness.

$\bar{u}$, which is inclined to lack purity in pronunciation.

CHAPTER VI

MUSICAL COMPREHENSION

The synthesis of responses—insuring proper posture and good diction—must include as one of its elements the factor of musical comprehension. This term designates the singer's alertness to the properties of the score, that quality of intelligence which enables him to use the directions and indications provided by the composer or the editor for assistance in performance. It further involves the performer's sensitivity to intangible considerations which are implicit in the musical fabric but cannot be set down in factual terminology or actual musical symbols. The student of singing must be aware of the necessity of taking from the score a diversity of implications. All too many individuals feel that the score has been learned if the singer can reproduce the indicated pitch relationships and time-values accurately. Actually, this is only the beginning, the point of departure for excursion into the real content of the work.

Comprehension of the score involves most obviously phrasing, intervallic relations, time-values, dynamic signs, and marks of expression. The singer must train himself to the point where he can look at a score and take in the details of the musical landscape in a quick over-all view. The first scrutiny should enable him to form a general conception just as a panoramic view of a countryside gives a general feeling for the scene. All the parts of the picture may not fall into exact position immediately; that relationship may have to be worked out through study of the scene, but at least a perspective, even though hazy, should result from the first examination.

Just as in building up the synthesis of responses involved in physical preparation it was necessary to concentrate upon separate items in order and then combine them as soon as possible, so, in building up a comprehension of the score, first, individual principles must be learned and im-

64

mediately combined. As soon as possible, all the factors involved in comprehending the score must operate at once, though they probably will best be acquired step by step in the beginning.

The first factor involved is awareness of phrase design. This design constitutes the basis of the musical work, and upon it the entire structure rests. Awareness of the structural aspect of the work is essential to any real understanding of its character.

In vocal music, the musical phrase is ordered by the grammatical phrase. The singer should acquire the habit of looking for the phrase unit in any new music; such units are determined by the thought groupings of the text. The performer should ascertain the groupings into which the words fall by virtue of their thought content. If the piece is well written, the singer is safe in using the phrase design of the text as a guide in determining the musical design.

Often the phrasing is indicated through markings provided by the composer or the editor. These markings occasionally conflict with the strict grammatical phrase. Nevertheless, if the indicated scheme seems to be a logical and musical one, it should be followed. In many cases varying interpretations regarding the phraseology will be possible. Decision as to the design to be executed must be made carefully, according to principles of literary sense as well as the demands of the musical structure. If an adjustment must be made between literary and musical values, the accommodation should be in favor of the musical phraseology. However, if the accommodation is so extreme as to throw the work out of balance, then that composition had best be abandoned as unsuitable for use.

The phrase design must be delineated by the singer with reference to (a) articulation, (b) contour. By articulation is meant the clear separation of phrases. It implies the execution of the design with such clarity that the structure of the work is revealed through precise treatment of the constituent phrase units. For the choral group, this demands exactness in attack and release. The first note of the phrase must be sounded simultaneously in all voices and the concluding note be released with equal precision. Diction enters here as a factor of prime importance. The first vowel sound must be uttered by all participating parts at the same instant. If the vowel is preceded by a consonant, still greater care is necessary for the simultaneous attack. It is, as a general rule, careless treatment of the initial consonant that is responsible for faulty attack. This consonant, sounded simultaneously throughout the chorus, must be of minimum duration unless some special descriptive effect requires extending it. Such effects, of course, are comparatively rare and should not be allowed to intrude into literature where they would be out of character.

As with the attack, it is usually a troublesome consonantal sound that causes difficulty at the release. The latter, too, should occur at precisely the same moment in all parts; consonants in final position customarily should be of minimum duration and definite in enunciation.

Between the attack and the release there should be an uninterrupted flow of tone through the final note of the phrase. This demands on the part of the singer the ability to produce a pure legato line, which is made possible by solidity of breath support and constancy of breath supply. It demands the continuous flow of breath from the diaphragm to the resonating cavities.

Here, again, a synthesis of responses is necessary. Legato is affected by the quality of the physical reactions involving breath support and also by the character of the enunciation and the vowel production. Not only must the breath be supplied evenly and steadily, but if legato is to be attained, the vowels must be sung fully and roundly with the vowel stream unimpeded by exaggerated enunciation of the consonants. The consonant should ride on the stream of the vowel tone, not interrupt it.

The production of a legato line is so nearly universal a principle of choral performance that this principle assumes the character of a generalization. Departures are to be made from it for *(a)* specific interpretative effects, *(b)* exceptional stylistic purposes, and *(c)* unusual rhythmic devices. These exceptions may take the form of *(a)* staccato passages, *(b)* dynamic accents, and *(c)* marcato effects.

The second aspect of phrase design has to do with the contour of the individual phrase, its curve or quality of line. This curve is determined by the relationship of textual accentuation to musical setting. Every phrase has at least one primary accent, that is, one point of high interest. This point is determined by the textual values, and, if the piece is well set, will be accorded comparable musical importance. Musical emphasis is not always brought about by application of accent or dynamic intensity. It may be achieved through harmonic stress; it may be brought about by manipulation of melodic line. No matter how attained, in a work that exhibits a happy union of text and music, the primary accent at the point of high interest in the text will coincide with one of equal interest in the musical setting.

In addition to the primary accent, every phrase will contain at least one, and possibly more, secondary accents. It is the number and sequential ordering of primary and secondary accents that determines the contour of the phrase. Failure to provide such treatment reduces the line to a flat level of dull monotony.

The learning process should begin with a consideration of the basic phrase design of the work at hand. To begin with the individual intervallic relationships, and from them attempt to build up the phrase design, is to start building a house by assembling the individual bricks before determining the plan of the structure. Only after the phrase design has been evolved, should attention be given to smaller points where difficulty may have arisen. It is for this reason that the conductor, in introducing the work, should plan to present the composition, or a section of it, in its entirety in order that the group may secure a feeling for the work as a whole. He probably will vary his presentation from time to time, so that every work is not introduced in identical fashion. He may have the work played by the accompanist; he may have the singers read it through as best they can if it is not too difficult; but he will strive to give them a view of at least one large section as a whole.

Following the first presentation, the phrase articulation for the various sections should be worked out, with attention at the same time to the contour of individual phrases. Meanwhile many fairly difficult intervallic relationships will take care of themselves. Intervals and time-values which the chorus continues to perform incorrectly should before long be isolated and cleared up, but only after they have been seen in relation to the work as a total unity.

While he is working out phrasing, pitch, and time relationships, the singer also should take note of the dynamic signs. There is no need for the singer to learn first the notes and time-values, as is all too often the customary procedure, and then, late in the process, apply the dynamic scheme after the composition is fairly well mastered in other respects. The dynamic scheme is an integral part of the musical structure (if the composer has written well), and the performer should attempt to reproduce its pattern as knowledge of the other aspects of the score is being developed.

Similarly, expression marks and performance instructions should be followed as they occur in the score without the director's drawing attention to them. The singer should have sufficient comprehension of notational symbols and sufficient apprehension of their implications to re-create the work as indicated. He should not be obliged to rely solely on the director for the interpretational scheme, which he can perfectly well develop for himself to a certain degree.

The director's task is to train his group in the beginning so that his own efforts may afterwards be conserved for more significant use than the translation of obvious symbols. It does not demand any rare gift of musical talent or exceptional mental endowment on the part of the singer to develop for himself an awareness of the implications of the score.

One must, however, apply his general intelligence with concentration to achieve success in this direction.

It may be granted that the terminology and system of musical signs customarily employed in music printing are only indications, not to be followed rigorously as representations of inflexible rules. It is to be conceded that in many cases their precise interpretation is the director's responsibility. Their exact meaning may not always be clear, and clarification may have to be provided by him. Nevertheless, an infinite amount of rehearsal can be saved if the singer learns to follow more or less automatically the suggestions given on the written page with any departures therefrom being indicated by the conductor as rehearsals proceed.

It may well be that the director does not agree with the markings indicated. It is his ultimate privilege to settle upon his own individual scheme of interpretation. In fact, it is not only his prerogative but his obligation to do so. He must be free to read the work as he feels it as long as his reading constitutes a logical and artistic expression. It is a comparatively simple matter for the director to indicate that in certain passages he would prefer, for instance, a forte in place of the mezzo-forte indicated by the score, or that he would like a less heavily marked accent than one for which the score calls. It is much easier to change an existing scheme than to start with no scheme at all and be in the position of having to indicate every dynamic color and every change of tempo which the composition demands.

Singers, as a whole, are particularly prone to carelessness in regard to the following elements of notation and terminology:

a. Time Problems.

  1. *Change of pattern.* Most singers need to pay closer attention to reproducing the mathematically correct relationship of the notes, particularly in the event of a shift in the pattern of time-values. When one metric pattern recurs sequenti-

ally and then is changed, singers all too often continue using the first.

2. *Dotted notes.* The pattern involving the dotted note followed by a note of shorter duration is seldom reproduced with accuracy. There is often a tendency to slight the first and give too much time to the second.

3. *Subdivision of the beat.* The difference between the pattern involving the subdivision of the pulse into two equal parts and that of a dotted value followed by a shorter one should be carefully noted. (See pp. 00).

4. *Subdivision of a value into three equal parts (the triplet).* For example, the pattern ♩♩♩ is often performed ♩♩·♩ so that the second note of the triplet is prolonged unduly and the last note slighted.

5. *Rests.* The rest has a value peculiar to itself and is an organic factor in the musical design. It is not merely a moment of dead silence, but a vital constituent of the total rhythmic movement. It should receive the exact mathematical value indicated for it by the score.

b. Pitch Problems.

1. *Half-steps.* Singers are particularly weak in the recognition of the half-step as an interval. The intelligent singer must so develop his powers of apprehension that he instantly differentiates between the half-step and the whole-step in his reading and reproduces each interval properly.

2. *Major and minor thirds.* The beginning singer is notoriously lax in his differentiation of the third as to minor or major quality. He must be particu-

larly accurate in the intonation of these two intervals.

c. Dynamic Signs. Dynamic signs are customarily ignored, even by singers of considerable experience.

1. *Lower dynamic levels.* The signs calling for pianissimo and pianississimo are particularly slighted.

2. *Diminuendo.* The diminuendo is seldom respected by the average singer. Great exactitude should be practiced in the reproduction of the dynamic scheme with particular respect to the ebb and flow of the tonal volume.

3. *Accent marks.* The accent mark is usually accorded little deference by the singer, though, as a matter of fact, it should be regarded with great concern. Very few choral groups can be depended upon to reproduce any of the various accentual effects with accuracy unless specifically instructed to do so by the director.

d. General Notational Signs.

1. *Repeat signs.* Many singers do not even see the repeat marks upon a first reading of the score. This is usually a fault of negligence, rather than of ignorance.

2. *Fermata signs.* Many choral groups have a tendency to sing straight through the fermata.

3. *Articulation of slurs.* In patterns requiring the execution of more than one tone to a single syllable of text, there is a common tendency to run the individual tones together. The singer must take care that each individual note in the pattern is clearly articulated and that each is given its due importance. The shorter the note value, the

more care must be exercised for proper articulation.

4. *Staccato marks.* The dot above the note calling for a staccato tone is customarily disregarded in the reading of the score.

e. Text.

1. *Meaning.* Singers often do not read the text as intelligently as they should with regard to thought content and sentence structure. There is a prevalent tendency to read the text syllable-by-syllable, rather than in phrase units or thought groupings. Words are misread and faults in pronunciation are committed that could have been avoided had the singer looked ahead and noted the proper position of the syllable within the word or, in some cases, of the word within the phrase.

2. *Phrase units.* The singer should establish the habit of perceiving the text in terms of phrase length and apprehending the individual phrase as a whole.

CHAPTER VII

PSYCHOLOGICAL ATTITUDE

Not only must the physical organism be in a proper state of preparation and the musical intelligence alert as to the implications of the score, but also the psychological attitude of the individual must be taken into account. Again, this is not something separate and apart from other factors of the singing process. Successful accomplishment in any aspect of study is conditioned to a high degree by the state of mind with which the student approaches the problem. However, there are certain elements in the psychological attitude that may be isolated for purposes of emphasis. The state of mind, first of all, must be that of responsiveness, of willingness on the part of the singer to make of himself an instrument by which the music may be made meaningful both to the listener and to himself as participant. It is essentially a matter of flexibility, operative in many different ways. It is of particular moment with reference to interpretation, which cannot be dissociated from the mental state of the performer. In developing interpretation, the approach should be through a consideration of the words. Upon first reading the text, the singer should strive to obtain a feeling for content and inner meaning. He must be imbued with the spirit of the utterance and must be able to transmit it to the listener. He must rid himself of all self-consciousness and must eliminate any individual personal reticence. He must give himself up to the basic implications of the work, allowing himself to go with the dramatic and emotional current of text and music.

This desired emotional and psychological freedom is a state not always easily obtainable. The modern person, and particularly the modern American person, has a dread of appearing sentimental, a reluctance to exhibit his inner feeling. Psychological responsiveness is possible only when the individual has become so thoroughly absorbed in what

73

the work has to say that all thought of self vanishes. This absorption is to be realized, not through deliberate seeking for self-abnegation and cultivated avoidance of self-consciousness, but through such saturation with the spirit and meaning of the work as will leave no room for self-contemplation.

Not only must the choral singer be sensitive to the interplay of emotional currents in text and music; he also must be responsive to the activity of the group with which he is performing. Each individual member of the organization must so integrate his own personality with that of the other members that all react as one. Here technique is combined with psychological responsiveness. Precision of attack, simultaneity of release, uniformity in consonantal enunciation—these result from a unanimity of physical reaction among all the members of the group. Blend and balance of tone, homogeneity of vowel color, are possible only when the individual personal activity is made a part of a larger group activity.

The individual singer must, furthermore, be willing to be responsive to the directions of the conductor. He must be ready to adopt new tempi, to regulate tonal volumes, to enter, in short, into the scheme by which the conductor attempts to set forth the work as an artistic unity.

A particularly important factor of the psychological attitude is that of aural consciousness, previously discussed. The cultivation of skill in listening is intrinsically a psychological matter. The singer must at all times be aurally aware as to what is going on. He must hear his own voice and his neighbor's. He must be able to blend his voice with that of his neighbor and, further, with that of the whole group. He must be aurally conscious at all times of the quality of *(a)* his own voice, *(b)* his neighbor's voice in the section, *(c)* the section of which he is a member, *(d)* the ensemble tone of the group as a whole. A well-developed aural consciousness is the most essential component in the development of good ensemble. It is imperative for blend of quality and for uniformity in vowel production. It is indispensable in obtaining clarity of consonantal enunciation. It is through a habit of concentrated listening that the singer should know when the chord is perfectly balanced and the various harmonic constituents are in a satisfactory relationship to each other. Similarly, it should be his ear which notifies him of the existence of a lack of equilibrium between the harmonic constituents.

It is upon aural consciousness more than upon any other single factor that intonation depends, a lack of concentrated listening being most often the cause of poor intonation. If the singer can actively hear the tone, he can usually sing it in tune. An alert aural consciousness, to be sure, is not the only prerequisite to correct intonation. Once again the synthesis of responses involved in singing is apparent. For good intonation, it is imperative that the breath stream proceed in an uninterrupted flow from the diaphragm through the trunk and chest into the resonating cavities; vowel production must be characterized by purity of quality and roundness of formation; most important of all, however, these factors must be combined with a habit of aural concentration. The singer must never allow the vigilance of his ear to relax; he must at all times be possessed of an alert aural awareness.

Feeling for rhythmic continuity is basically a psychological matter. It involves on the part of the singer a sensitivity to the fundamental motion underlying all music, and the ability to maintain at all times the rhythmic vitality of the work at hand. The beginning singer is inclined to confuse rhythm with meter; that is, he is prone to expect a succession of pulses whose pattern or organization is determined by the alternation of strong and weak beats in a more or less regular succession. It is possible for music to possess a clear rhythmic definition and yet, at the same time, to be devoid of strong metrical feeling. Witness Gregorian chant, which has fluidity and continuousness of rhythmic movement but is mostly wanting in regularity of metrical organization. A lack of adherence to metrical patterning is observable in the music of the various madrigal schools, in which the rhythmic movement is conditioned by the necessities of the prose rhythms. When the text is metrical in character, a metrical effect is customarily to be noted in the music; when the text is non-metrical—in so-called free rhythm—the music is likely to proceed in similar fashion, without being under the circumscription of confining the rhythmic movement within regularly recurring measures of identical length, a characteristic procedure in certain later eras.

The singer must be aware of the implicitness of rhythmic movement and, whatever the basis of its conception, must so perform the work that the quality of rhythmic continuity is preserved. The rhythmic pulse is set in motion with the first note of the work and must not be impeded until it has finished its course with the conclusion of the final note of the composition. The pulse may hasten or slacken, but it must never come to a dead halt. Even at a fermata there must be a sense of the expectation of further movement to follow.

The sense of rhythmic continuity must be maintained also between the various sections of a work. The cadence of the section within the larger movement should bear a rhythmic relation to whatever has preceded and likewise to what follows. It should not possess the finality of a concluding cadence unless it actually constitutes the close of the movement. The correct treatment of the rests, mentioned earlier on p. 70, depends to a great degree upon the singer's psychological awareness of their rhythmic significance. They are important bits of mosaic in the rhythmic pattern. To rob them of their proper duration is to destroy the cohesiveness and clarity of the design. The rests must be endowed with a sense of rhythmic continuity, bearing an intimate relation to the sounds which precede and those which follow.

Precision of ensemble is largely dependent upon the feeling of the group for rhythmic continuity, with the feeling of the individual singer integrated with that of the other

members of the organization. There should be such a unanimity of response throughout the group that all members
react at the precisely identical moment. This again is principally a matter of suppleness and flexibility, an essentially
psychological consideration. So also with simultaneity of
release, which is particularly often subject to careless
treatment. Clarity in releasing the word, in enunciating the
final consonant, and especially in releasing the final consonant of a phrase, is usually the result of a unified psychological attitude on the part of the group. A sharper definition
of the release is usually brought about by directing the
singers to endow the release with rhythmic vitality.

To re-create fine literature, one must be psychologically
awake to its values and implications. Further, one must communicate its message in terms of its own vocabulary and
with respect for the idiom of its utterance. Excellence of
performance is necessary. It is to be assumed in the presentation of any work. But one must go beyond mere excellence
of production. One must do more than sing with good diction,
with respect for the structural demands of the work, with the
supplying of adequate breath to the tone and with skill in
the delineation of line. Fine technique is not enough. One
must re-create the work in terms of its own style. A consideration of the elements that go to make up the style and
the implications of the style for choral performance will
serve as the basis of discussion for Part Two of this work.

PART TWO

Style

CHAPTER VIII

FUNDAMENTAL DETERMINANTS OF STYLE

It is a valid assertion that music has achieved its ultimate purpose only when it is brought to life through performance. The musician who maintains this belief and seeks to put it into practice is confronted at the outset by the problem of proper presentation. The matter revolves around what in musical parlance is termed "interpretation." An attempt is here made to consider those elements that help to make up the interpretative process, for the purpose of arriving at an understanding of the factors that determine interpretative style. It is the further purpose of the subsequent discussion to consider the problem of interpretation as it relates to the performance of choral literature and to evolve a set of principles which may act as a guide in developing an interpretative scheme appropriate to a particular work.

What are the components that should influence a conductor in evolving an interpretative scheme for a given work? What are the considerations to be taken into account in developing a reading of the score that is logical and reveals to the listener the inner content?

One of the supreme accolades of the musical world is a tribute stating that a performance has been presented with a fine sense of style. On the other hand, no criticism is more censorious than one asserting that a performance has been stylistically inappropriate. Of what is style made? And how is a conductor to know what has in one case merited the praise of stylistic appropriateness and in another elicited the condemnation that there has been a lack of feeling for style?

These questions lead to a consideration of the basic meaning of the word "style" itself. Webster defines it as follows:

Mode of expressing thought in language, . . . esp., such use of language as exhibits the spirit and faculty of an artist; characteristic mode of expression, . . .

79

> Distinctive or characteristic mode of presenta-
> tion, construction, or execution in any art, employ-
> ment, or product, esp. in any of the fine arts; . . .
> Manner or method of acting or performing; . . .[6]

It is to be observed that the word has a double connotation. Basically it has reference to the "characteristic mode of expression" on the part of the creator, which means, in the musical work, the individually distinctive fashion in which the composer presents his ideas. It indicates a way of writing peculiar to a specific composer or to groups of composers who may be considered related by reason of some particular affinity of circumstance or spirit. When the composers of a group are virtually contemporaneous and motivated by similar ideals and purposes, the group is said to constitute a school.

The category to which the term is applied may be any one of several. For instance, a style may be said to be characteristic of a particular person, as when one speaks of "the Bach style" or "the style of Palestrina." It may be said to be characteristic of a chronological or historical period, as when one speaks of "nineteenth-century style" or when one employs the phrase "the style of the Baroque Era," referring to seventeenth- and eighteenth-century compositions. The term may indicate a manner common to geographic or national groups as in the case of "the style of the North Germans," "the French style," and so on. It may be applied to the texture of the score, as when one speaks of "polyphonic" or "harmonic" style; to the medium of performance, as in "pianistic" or "vocal style"; or to the form, as in the case of "oratorio style," "operatic style," "madrigal style."

Style, however, has an aspect that extends beyond the initial creative process. It has to do also with the re-creation, on the performer's part, of the composer's original idea. That is, it embraces a second creative process, which

---

6 *New International Dictionary of the English Language;* 2nd edition unabridged, Springfield, Mass., Merriam, 1947, cop. 1945, p. 2505.

is brought about by the interpreter. A duality of concept arises from the crystallization of thought in a certain form by the composer and the manner of treatment accorded that thought-form by the interpreter. Yet so closely related are style in interpretation and style in composition that the true artist cannot separate them.

The whole art of interpretation consists essentially of the re-creation of the composer's idea and of its transmission to the listener in terms of the performer's perception of inner meaning. Thus interpretation depends upon the performer's understanding of the composer's intent, upon his comprehension of the basic implications of the work and his ability to convey these perceptions to the listener. His skill in translating the composer's idea in terms of his own reactions defines his accomplishment as an interpretative artist.

If the interpretative artist is to re-create the composer's idea properly, he must know what modes of thought and types of expression are peculiar to the composer, what distinguishes this composer's style from that of others, and what is common to other composers of the period or school. In other words, his performance must be formulated with strict respect for the composer's manner of speech; his reading of the score must be consistent with the musical language of its creator.

This is not to deny the element of personal expressiveness. Interpretation after all is a matter of personal creativeness, and to deny the personal element is to deny the act of interpretation itself. The aim of the interpreter should not necessarily be to submerge his own personality in that of the composer; nor should it be to glorify himself at the other's expense. Rather, it should be to unite with the composer in developing a total artistic product.

In order to arrive at an understanding of the style of a composer, one should take into account his personality and temperament. To be sure, there sometimes seems to be a marked cleavage between the character of a composer's music and his own character, as this is revealed by a study of his biography. But, more often than not, the two things very obviously correspond. Is the composer a person of sober and serious disposition? Then much of his music is likely to be in a similar sober vein. Is he philosophic and contemplative by nature? If so, his work is apt often to be of a profound and meditative character. Is he of a gay and lively spirit? Then a substantial part of his music will probably tend toward buoyancy and animation.

The composer's technical equipment assumes great importance as a determinant of style. At the outset there is the phenomenon of native endowment. What is the degree of talent possessed by the composer in question? Is he merely gifted or does he have that divine spark which makes him a genius towering above his fellows? Further, how has this native endowment been developed? What is the state of his proficiency? His skill as contrapuntist, his deftness in dealing with harmonic materials, his aptness in instrumentation and scoring, all the diverse aspects of the technique of composition, together with that innate quality of inspiration indefinable in technical terms alone, are significant ingredients in determining a composer's style.

What Ferdinand Praeger refers to as "the state of the grammar of the Art"[7] also plays a role in molding individual style. The composer is affected not only by his own technical dexterity but also by the characteristics of the musical technique of his day. Each period has a tendency to attach particular importance to certain aspects of music, occasionally at the expense of others. In the Renaissance, for instance, counterpoint was the characteristic mode of expression, with comparatively little emphasis on harmony as such. The nineteenth century, on the other hand, was inclined toward a preoccupation with harmonic effects, often with slight regard for the contrapuntal element. Composers of a particular period frequently have exhibited great facility

---

7 "Style," *Musical Association Proceedings*, 12th session, 1885-1886, pp. 93-94.

in dealing with certain forms and media while evidencing little skill in or concern with others. Perfect knowledge of style presupposes an understanding of the technical ideals of the period and of the forms through which the musical thought of the day found expression.

An additional factor affecting the formulation of style is provided by geographical and national influences. Every nation, every racial group seems to demonstrate a predilection for a certain cast of thought and for a distinctive manner of statement. The Germanic peoples, for example, seem disposed toward solemnity of utterance and seriousness of purpose. The philosophic note is sounded through all German art and life and makes itself strongly felt in much Germanic music. The French, on the other hand, are a more realistic people, tending to look at things in a thoroughly practical way. A logic of thought, free from deep emotional implications, is reflected in all forms of Gallic art and makes its imprint upon French music, which in general proceeds upon a rationalistic basis.

A further determinant of style lies in the character of the society in which the creative artist lives and works. What are the conditions of the historical and social background? The temper of the thought of the day, the place of religion in the life of the times, the degree of economic ease or stringency, the social manners and customs, the stratification of society and the relationship existing between social classes, all these affect the composer and his style of writing. Each epoch has its own special traits and its own tone. To understand the work of art one must have an understanding of the quality of life within the era in which it was produced. To quote the composer-critic C. H. H. Parry:

> . . . style is either gratifying or repulsive in proportion to its just relation to its conditions. There is a technique of life also, as well as of art, and the style of every section of society varies in accordance with its conditions; and the outcome of

attempts to adopt a style belonging to one branch of society in a branch of society whose conditions of life are altogether different is a familiar form of what is called vulgarity . . . .

The worst fault in style is the mixing up of types which are especially apt to different groups of conditions, different situations, and different attitudes of mind. A perfect work of art is a perfectly organized presentation of an original unity. If grapes are found on one bough and figs on another, men may guess that it is a sham. The perfect adaptation to conditions entails perfect unity of style, and it may be inferred conversely that complete perfection of style is to be found not in intrinsic qualities but in perfect and relevant consistency.[8]

The determinants of an individual composer's style, then, may be summarized as follows:

a. Personality and temperament.

b. Technical equipment.

c. "The state of the grammar of the art."

d. Geographical and national group affiliation.

e. Historical and social background.

For the purpose of the interpreter these factors may be examined in reverse order. Attention will be given first to historical periods and geographical influences, and thereafter to individual aspects of technique with reference to choral literature.

---

8 *Style in Musical Art,* London, Macmillan, 1911, pp. 2, 17.

CHAPTER IX

HISTORICAL PERIODS AND GEOGRAPHICAL INFLUENCES

In order properly to interpret works from the choral literature, the conductor must first have a knowledge of the great historic periods. This is fundamental in arriving at an understanding of the background of the individual composition. It is granted that no clear line of demarcation can be drawn between the various periods. Each flows gradually into the next, dissolving, as it were, into the succeeding epoch. The declining days of one era are usually the dawn of a new one. However, for convenience, the great historical periods may be indicated roughly as follows:

a. Renaissance, 1425-1600. It is in the Renaissance that a many-voiced choral literature may be said to have its origin. Choral polyphony as a style of writing comes into existence in the fifteenth century, notably in the music of the Northern French school, the leaders of which were Guillaume Dufay, *c.* 1400-1474, and Gilles Binchois, *c.* 1400-1460. Prior to that time choral music was essentially plainsong, in which all voices are employed on a unisonal melodic line. Vocal part-music before the early fifteenth century was intended to be sung by groups of soloists. The Renaissance comes to a climax in Italy with some of the work of the great visitor from the North, Roland de Lassus (perhaps better known under the Italian form of his name: Orlando di Lasso), 1530/1532-1594; with the Roman school of Palestrina, 1524/1525-1594, and of the temporarily resident Spaniard, Victoria, *c.* 1549-1611; and with the Venetian school of the Gabrielis (Andrea Gabrieli, *c.* 1510-1586; Giovanni Gabrieli, 1557-1612). In England the Elizabethan madrigal school brings the period to a close.

b. Baroque, 1600-1750. A change in the current of musical thought is evident around the year 1600 with the new monodic style of the Florentine Camerata, whose leaders were Count Giovanni Bardi, 1534-1612, Count Jacopo Corsi,

85

born *c.* 1560, the poet Ottavio Rinuccini, 1562-1621, and the musicians Vincenzo Galilei, *c.* 1520-1591, Giulio Caccini, *c.* 1546-1618, Jacopo Peri, 1561-1633, and Emilio del Cavalieri, *c.* 1550-1602. Coming shortly thereafter in point of time, Claudio Monteverdi, 1567-1643, stands out as one of the great masters of the early Baroque. The era may be said to close with Johann Sebastian Bach, 1685-1750, and George Frideric Handel, 1685-1759.

c. Classicism, 1750-1825. The period of Josef Haydn, 1732-1809, Wolfgang Amadeus Mozart, 1756-1791, and Ludwig van Beethoven, 1770-1827, is that of the so-called classic era. Beethoven has been considered a "man of transition," in that he constitutes a bridge between Classicism and succeeding Romanticism. In him are to be found in somewhat more than usual measure traits constituting a link between past and future.

d. Romanticism. 1800-1900. Ushered in by Beethoven, early Romanticism is epitomized in the music of Carl Maria von Weber, 1786-1826, and Franz Schubert, 1797-1828. In Richard Wagner, 1813-1883, and Johannes Brahms, 1833-1897, are to be found aspects of late nineteenth-century Romanticism. Intermediate between early and late phases are Felix Mendelssohn, 1809-1847, Robert Schumann, 1810-1856, Frédéric Chopin, 1810-1849, and Franz Liszt, 1811-1886 — these among many other proponents of the Romantic spirit. The Romantic period corresponds roughly to the historical era of nationalistic expansion. The Romantic style was so widespread in its effect and so universally adopted by the practitioners of all the arts that the terms *Romanticism* and *Nineteenth-century Style* are employed interchangeably to indicate the characteristic expressional manner of the period.

e. Modern Period, 1875 to the present. Modern developments in music may be said to open with French Impressionism, which as a musical style appeared during the last quarter of the nineteenth century. Impressionism is regarded by some authorities as a late Romantic phenomenon and by others as the first phase of present-day Modernism. The existence of this disagreement illustrates the difficulty of making any categorical separation between historical periods. Following Impressionism and continuing down to the present there has been a more or less rapid succession of different movements, many of them related, known as Neo-classicism, Expressionism, Futurism, Realism, and so on. Chapters XI-XV will be devoted to a discussion of the various historical periods in greater detail.

•

The geographical and national factor has been mentioned previously as a significant determinant of style. One of the first elements to emerge in a consideration of this factor is that of language. The contour of a melodic line is greatly affected by the speech inflections of the tongue in question. Inflectional values vary from language to language — the rise and fall of the voice, the syllabic accent, the relative accentual relationships within the individual phrases. It has been said earlier that vocal music should be conceived as a perfect union of text and music, in which the most minute considerations of both language and tone interact upon each other with extreme potency.

The conditioning power of language appears first of all in rhythmic treatment. In a proper setting the rhythmic accents of the music coincide with the accentual values of the spoken text. The placing of a strong musical stress on an unimportant word is defined as *false accent* and is to be avoided as the archenemy of musical-poetic sensitivity. While some accommodation should be made in favor of the purely musical requirements, nevertheless it must be possible to bring the textual and musical accentuations into a reasonable balance, or else — as has already been said on p. 65 — the work in question had best be given up as a poor piece of writing.

With respect to interpretation, it may usually be taken for granted that the accentual scheme of the music will be in agreement with the conventional usages of the spoken language. The conductor will not place undue stress upon words of little significance merely to satisfy a preconceived rhythmic notion on his part; neither will he slight those words which merit accentual emphasis.

Because of differences between languages, translations are seldom satisfactory for singing. The melodic contour, formulated with regard to the necessities of one language, does not lend itself readily to the entirely dissimilar necessities of another. Italian vocal inflection will not often correspond to that of a German translation. French syllabic accentuation can be reproduced in English only with the greatest difficulty.

As indicated in the foregoing chapters, beauty of tone is determined by the quality of the vowel sounds. Consequently tone quality will be defined by the characteristic vowel sounds of the language employed. The choral director must be aware of the quality proper to the formations of the language with which he is dealing. He must not isolate tone from text but must adopt a standard of beauty that is in accord with the ideals of the language.

By way of summary, the singing requirements of a language include *(a)* a rhythmic scheme developed with due regard for accentual demands, *(b)* a molding of the melodic line conditioned by the inflectional curve of the spoken text, *(c)* tone production in relation to the vowel quality of the given language.

A survey of choral literature reveals that nationality has been an important agency not only in affecting the nature of textual-musical relationships but also with regard to the purely musical aspect of the score. Nationality exerts an influence particularly with reference to:

a. Manner of rhythmic treatment.

b. Character of the melodic-harmonic concept.

c. Degree of emotional expressiveness.

These seem to constitute the factors most strongly affected

by variations in treatment occasioned by the differing points of view and concepts of the several national schools. The remainder of this chapter will be devoted to the principal national styles with respect to these factors.

•

FRANCE

a. In observing the French style, one cannot fail to note that buoyancy of rhythmic feeling is a frequent characteristic throughout all the historic periods. One finds a metrical pulse lightly but definitely marked, a nimbleness of pace, and a continuity of rhythmic progress. The ballet has enjoyed wide popularity in France. The lightness and vivacity of that form are carried over into much French music.

b. It would appear that the French characteristically pay close attention to textual values in vocal music. The projection of the words with clarity and distinctness and the revelation of the dramatic content of the text have been through all the ages prime desiderata for the performance of French vocal music. The French vocal style in general has a tendency to assume a declamatory character, the melodic line closely following the contour of the spoken text.

Until the nineteenth century the Gallic composer tended to attach more importance to declamatory-rhythmic melody than to harmonic considerations. With the nineteenth century there emerges a new harmonic preoccupation, which is evident in France as well as the rest of the western world. The French Impressionism of Claude Debussy, 1862-1918, admittedly is a pre-eminently harmonic style, but this is a comparatively recent development viewed in the larger course of history.

c. French music in the main seems to avoid portraying any high degree of subjective emotion. The Gallic spirit is not customarily given to emotional probings. It has in the main a distaste for the public parading of inner stresses and strains, being more *raisonnable* in its depiction of emotional conflict. Rationality is the keynote of the Gallic attitude.

ITALY

a. The Italian style, like the French, is characterized by rhythmic lilt and vitality of motion. Even in slow, sustained passages a sense of rhythmic progression should be preserved. While this principle holds true for all choral literature, it is particularly evident in the fundamentally Italian style. The rhythmic patterns are of great variety, often piquant in design. The pulse is marked definitely, with rather more weight than in French music and rather less than in the German. The movement has a quality of rhythmic flow and an elasticity of step.

b. The most prominent trait of all Italian music, however, is its love of a melody which is essentially vocal in character. Soaring, curving melodic lines, spacious in contour and emotionally uninhibited, leap in abundance from the pages of Italian music. Melody is usually delineated with a careful regard for graciousness of line. The leading of the voice parts is generally smooth, without conspicuous disjunct motion. Fluency of progression is a natural result, successions of awkward or uncomfortable intervals seldom being encountered. Melody rather than harmony predominates in the typical Italian composition.

Vocal opulence is a vital necessity for this rich melodic utterance. Beauty of tone is to Italian music the breath of life. Even in projecting textual meaning, words are uttered with care for their purely sensuous aspect. For the Italian, it would seem that the word often exists primarily as a means for creating physical beauty and that through this beauty the implication of the text is to be conveyed. Communication of thought and feeling apparently is brought about as a result of physical loveliness. The French and German schools, in contrast, seem to emphasize transmission of thought content, with sensuous beauty issuing as a secondary consideration.

Striving for physical beauty is to be remarked again in the Italian absorption with proportion and arrangement. Clearness of form and symmetry of design are attributes of the best Italian art, no matter what the medium employed. Preoccupation with such considerations occasionally causes content to be sacrificed to an exaggerated emphasis on design.

The Italian concern with such matters demands that the director place great emphasis on production, on the *bel canto* ideal of beautiful tone *per se,* in order to realize the vocal excellence which is indispensable to the performance of Italian choral literature.

Another trait of the Italian is his fondness for decorative effects. Melodic lines are elaborated with all manner of *fioriture,* roulades and other embellishments. The correct treatment of the multitudinous ornamental devices constitutes a perpetual problem for the choral director. This is true not only of native Italian music but of many other works composed under its influence. Because of the widespread acceptance of Italian methods abroad, the practice of the application of ornamentation became universal, particularly during the seventeenth and eighteenth centuries. The following works in English are of particular assistance in the study of ornamentation:

> Putnam Aldrich, "Ornamentation," in *Harvard Dictionary of Music,* 1945.
> Putnam Aldrich, *Ornamentation in Bach's Organ Works,* published by Coleman-Ross, 1950.
> Edward Dannreuther, *Musical Ornamentation,* published by Novello and Company, 1891-1895.
> Arnold Dolmetsch, *The Interpretation of the Music of the XVIIth and XVIIIth Centuries,* published by Novello, 1915.
> *Grove's Dictionary of Music and Musicians,* "Ornaments."

The execution of ornaments demands knowledge of the

associated tradition on the conductor's part and presupposes well-established technique on the part of the singer. The smaller intervals so commonly occurring in ornamental devices require extreme care for true intonation; the rapidity of the roulade calls for the highest degree of flexibility; the necessity for cultivating the *bel canto* ideal of finesse is apparent.

c. With regard to emotional expressiveness, the salient factor in the Italian attitude is pliability. An essential facet of the Italian temperament is a readiness to accept the implications of the emotional undercurrent. There is no sense of struggling against it, as is often the case with the Germans for instance, nor is there the impression of standing aloof, regarding it from a point removed, as the French are prone to do. Rather there is the sense of going along with it. The interpreter of Italian music must possess the psychological suppleness that will make him responsive to the play of the emotions and must be able to communicate the interplay of dramatic and emotional forces to the listener.

Richness of vocal and melodic color, vitality of movement, freedom in emotional r e p r e s e n t a t i o n — these are essential to the proper performance of Italian music.

THE NETHERLANDS

In the course of music history a great impetus to the development of a truly choral style was provided by the masters who have been rather loosely termed the Netherlanders. The territory named "The Netherlands" in the sixteenth century covered present-day Holland, Belgium, and parts of northern France, so that the people called Netherlanders included not only Dutchmen, but also Flemings, Walloons, and Frenchmen. The difficulty of classifying composers from this area is obvious. There is a strong tendency among recent historians to classify the group to which Guillaume Dufay and Gilles Binchois belonged as Northern French (cf. p. 85) and their Renaissance successors in the area as simply Franco - Netherlandish. A less up - to - date grouping — but one that is to be found in much current literature and which offers the convenience, for present purposes, of a larger number of subdivisions for reference — is the following:

Burgundian: Guillaume Dufay, *c.* 1400-1474; Gilles Binchois, *c.* 1400-1460.

Flemish: Johannes Okeghem, *c.* 1420-1495; Jacob Obrecht (actually a Dutchman), *c.* 1450-1505; Heinrich Isaak, *c.* 1450-1517; Josquin Des Prez, *c.* 1450-1521; Adrian Willaert, *b.* between 1480 and 1490, *d.* 1562; Jacob Arcadelt, *c.* 1514-c. 1557; Roland de Lassus, 1530/1532-1594.

Franco-Flemish: Jean Mouton, *c.* 14 70-15 2 2; Antoine de Févin, *c.* 1473-1512; Nicolas Gombert, *c.* 1490-*c.* 1556/1566; Clemens non Papa (Jacobus Clemens), *c.* 1510-1555/1556.[9]

The various Flemish composers in particular have produced a great body of significant choral literature.

a. One of the most readily apparent trains of the Flemings is energy and decisiveness of rhythmic movement, their music for the most part abounding in physical vigor and vitality. The rhythmic pulse is emphatic and at the same time characterized by fluidity.

b. The Fleming appears to be less concerned with the intrinsically vocal or singable character of the melodic line than is the Italian. Flemish melodies are inclined to be bold in contour, often assuming an architectonic character. They exhibit a fondness for disjunct motion, frequently employing intervals which are not particularly comfortable to sing. A certain sense of angularity is a consequence of this lack of vocal concern, but, at the same time, there is a wonderful feeling of strength and power.

---

9 See article "Flemish School," *Harvard Dictionary of Music,* pp. 268-270; Also Gustave Reese, *Music in the Renaissance,* New York, W.W. Norton, 1954, Chapters I-III, V-IX; Paul Henry Lang, "The So-Called Netherlands Schools," *Musical Quarterly,* XXV (1939), 48-59.

Credit is ascribed to the Flemish writers for the development of one of the chief contrapuntal techniques: imitation. The music of the Netherlanders is predominantly horizontal in concept. The structure depends upon a combination of elements interlocked through the cohesive effect of independent and yet closely related contrapuntal constituents. All voices are conceived as equally important in the texture. Whatever harmonic implications occur are brought about by the coincidence of contrapuntal lines. Hence the use of the terms "coincidental" or "resultant" harmony to characterize this aspect of Flemish music.

  c. In determining the emotional tone of the music of the Flemish masters, it is to be noted that they reveal a proclivity for the devotional, showing an affiliation with the Germans in a contemplative and philosophical approach to life. The other-worldly preoccupation of the time is demonstrated in the ethereal and mystical quality of their religious music. Flemish secular music on the other hand shows an abandonment in the love of physical life, which to some individuals is distasteful as seeming to be coarse or gross in character. This love of physical life is a logical outcome of the thought attitudes of the period; it is to be appreciated only by the person who has taken the trouble to acquaint himself with the characteristics of the cultural epoch in which this music was created. Here as always music cannot be considered merely as music alone, but must be understood as a product of the life of its time. It proceeds out of life, and the performer of a later generation can convey its meaning to his contemporaries only if he has some ability to enter into the spirit of the times and to comprehend the vocabulary of its expression.

GERMANY

German music reflects the character of a people who seem by nature predisposed toward soberness of thought and deliberateness of action. The feeling of impressiveness, the sensation of vigor and of decisive movement, the solidarity and thickness of texture common to much German music, are traits which are not entirely unrelated to native attitudes of mind and characteristic modes of expression.

a. Germanic style is inclined toward a sturdy marking of the rhythmic pulsation, together with a comparatively regular definition of the metrical pattern during and following the Baroque period. Appreciation of the German proclivity for vigorous rhythmic pulse and for strong metrical successions is basic in evolving an interpretative scheme for the majority of the works of this school.

b. The previously discussed force of language in determining melodic contour is singularly evident in German vocal music, where melody often bears a particularly close relation to the text. The German school exhibits a particular tendency to treat the melody as a vehicle for the word-idea. Thus in contrast to the Italian accommodation of textual declamation to symmetry of melodic contour, it would seem that in typically German writing melodic arrangement frequently defers to transmission of thought and meaning. In other words, in German composition form is often governed by content, whereas the reverse is frequently true in Italian works, as has been remarked earlier.

German thought has a predilection for the speculative and contemplative. The German mind enjoys working out problems and developing ideas. The aptness of the Germans in working with musical form is one manifestation of this fundamental national attitude. Another is the addiction which the Germans have evidenced to the contrapuntal style. The latter is of all styles the most peculiarly intellectual in its demands, being essentially concerned with the manipulation of abstract musical material and offering a particular challenge to the inventive mind. It had been evident as a stylistic feature of the fifteenth-century Burgundian school of Dufay and of the succeeding Flemish schools of Okeghem, Obrecht, and Des Prez, as mentioned above. The principle was taken up by the fifteenth- and sixteenth-century German composers,

Heinrich Finck, 1445-1527, Paul Hofhaimer, 1459-1537, and Thomas Stoltzer, *c.* 1480-1526, and zealously practiced by them. Even when seventeenth-century monody had all but obliterated counterpoint in a great part of the musical world, the Germans never entirely forsook the contrapuntal tradition.

The harmonic implications usually are strong in typically German music. The German apparently likes a fabric which is tightly woven, thick in texture, with a feeling of strength and solidity in the harmonic underpinning. He customarily prefers a rich harmonic palette with variety in coloristic combinations. Not only the conductor, but also the singer of German choral music must have an understanding of harmonic structure. He must be able to sense the warmth, richness, and solidity of the texture, and must be able to relate his own part to those of the remaining voices in such a way that a compact, well-knit fabric results.

c. As regards emotional expressiveness, in the typically German composition the word-idea should usually be infused with a quality of personal feeling. This is to be contrasted with what appears at times to be a purely rationalistic statement of the idea in the essentially French work. The German melodic line often seems to become, as it were, a channel through which there may be released inner, subjective feeling and thought. Experiencing things deeply and profoundly, the representative German seems disposed toward fervor of emotional utterance, particularly when the thought revolves around a more or less serious problem; consequently a certain warmth of expression should customarily characterize the treatment of the essentially Germanic choral piece.

ENGLAND

a. English style is characterized by freshness and vigor of rhythmic feeling. The pulse is defined sturdily, being somewhat less ponderous than in German music and rather more decided than in music of the French school.

Although a work may be quiet and contemplative in nature, there customarily should be a sense of continuity of movement and an urgency of progression. The particularly intimate connection between the rhythmic contours of English art music and those of the national folk music deserves special comment. This connection may be perceived in the healthy, "out-of-doors" quality of English rhythmic movement, which carries with it the suggestion of a close affinity with the soil of the English countryside.

b. The melodic line of English music is direct and straightforward. The molding of the musical phrase exhibits the strong influence exercised by purely musical considerations, with an equilibrium maintained between the attraction of the dramatic-emotional element on the one hand and that of the abstract musical idea on the other. The word-idea of English music, although set forth with clarity and distinctness, lacks the emphatically declamatory manner of the German and the French styles. While the sense of the word is conveyed with due regard for meaning, the delivery is inclined to be matter-of-fact and self-contained, with understatement rather than any suggestion of overstatement.

The harmonic palette of the English school is in general cool in tone. There is no excessive preoccupation with harmonic structure, which as a usual matter is conceived in terms of its relation to the melodic line and seems in a way to proceed from it.

c. The English spirit much of the time has been an essentially calm one. Inclined to be less volatile in emotional manifestation than the people of southern Europe and less concerned with the problems of inner struggle than the Germans, the English have a tendency to proceed on a more nearly even keel. In dramatic expression the emotional shades are of a comparatively neutral color, lacking in general the warm accents of Italian melody and missing altogether in the starkness of the typically Russian mood representation.

The English are inclined to be less concerned with pure-

ly sensuous beauty than are the Italians. While the word-idea
is presented simply and in such a way that it seems understated, it is never allowed to become submerged in purely
musical or physical effect. A careful balance is usually
preserved between the various constituent elements. The
production of beautiful tone as such seldom assumes the
importance it often has for the Italians. Neither does the
declamation of the word-idea disregard the acoustical demands of the ear. Rather, there is a well-modulated assertion
of the central thought, controlled in nature, whose manner
of statement is determined by the requirements of the musical structure. The score is discreet in tone. "Passionate vio-
lence of intervals or rhythm or accents are unknown to it" [10]

RUSSIA

The Russians did not enter the field as important con-
tributors to choral repertoire until the nineteenth century.
At that time an awakening interest in Russian art and life
in general began to turn the eyes of the world in the direction
of Russia as a significant musical entity. Since then the
widespread performance of Russian choral music — and
particularly of Russian liturgical music — has made it imperative to recognize the Russians among those whose contribution to choral literature constitutes a noteworthy
achievement.

a. An inclination toward extravagance appears to be a
basic trait of the Russian temperament. Overstatement is
frequently manifested in the unremitting rhythmic activity of
the typical Russian score. The movement is seldom relaxed,
rhythmic tension being evident even in passages of a comparatively calm and meditative nature. Joined with the love
of rhythmic energy is a fondness for the extremes of the
tempo range. Fast tempos tend to be exceedingly fast; slow
tempos incline toward excessive slowness. Not only are

---

10 Parry, *Style in Musical Art*, p. 157.

the extremes of the rhythmic range employed; they are found in close juxtaposition, abrupt alternations between passages of varying degrees of rhythmic intensity frequently being encountered. The contrast obtained by these sudden tempo alternations is responsible for the particularly dramatic tone of much Russian music.

The suggestion of exaggeration provided by intensification of the rhythmic pulsation and by the employment of the extremes of the tempo range is not the only distinguishing mark of Russian rhythmic treatment. The Russian also favors the effect produced by the organization of meter into patterns which to the Western mind seem to produce irregularity of contour. Western composers tend to organize rhythmic pulsations into meters of two or three beats ($\frac{2}{4}$, $\frac{2}{2}$, $\frac{3}{4}$, $\frac{3}{2}$, etc.) or of their multiples ($\frac{4}{4}$, $\frac{9}{8}$, etc.). The Russian feels no such circumscription. He not only employs duple and triple meters together with their multiples, but also draws freely on other successions, exhibiting particular delight in five- and seven-pulse measures. He further enjoys the effect provided by the use of multiple meters, the combination of a series of different groupings within the same phrase unit. The organization of rhythm in this fashion imparts a quality of exoticism and a rhythmic tang which the non-Russian often finds engaging.

b. Such rhythmic devices naturally affect the melodic contour. On first acquaintance the melodies, often irregular in length, may strike the listener as formless. Again it is essential to regard the musical work in the light of the environmental factors, human and otherwise, that have helped to shape it. Once one comes to know the components of the Russian style, what at first appeared formless and unpolished suddenly becomes a thoroughly logical and intelligible expression.

The modal character of Russian music is another conspicuous melodic feature. The old modes lingered in Russia after most of the rest of Europe had succumbed to the principles of major-minor scale construction, and for that reason have permeated a large portion of its choral literature. The intonation of modal intervals, especially when occurring in conjunction with diatonic scale material, constitutes a problem of considerable difficulty for the average singer. The choral director must take particular care to obtain accurate intonation in such passages.

Russian choral music for the most part is characterized by rhythmic-harmonic rather than contrapuntal interest. This apparent preference for harmony above counterpoint may have arisen because of the fact that by the time Russian choral music appeared as an important body of repertoire, in other words, by the nineteenth century, the musical world was almost entirely preoccupied with harmonic considerations and counterpoint as a rule was relegated to a subordinate role. The harmonic aspect of the typically Russian choral work is inclined toward solidity of structure and richness of color, this color being due partly to the impact of native musical materials and partly to the interaction of Russian and Western European influences, which during the nineteenth century were extending and expanding the harmonic vocabulary.

 c. Emotional expressiveness with the Russian in general means dramatic intensification of the prevailing mood. The emotional tone is frequently highlighted to an extreme degree and the dramatic conflicts are often brought into a struggle of terrific intensity. The conflict may be one in which the composer seems to plunge directly so that it appears to be viewed from near at hand, as in Tchaikovsky's personal introspection; or it may be a struggle regarded from a point afar, as in the somewhat objective contemplation with which Mussorgsky seems to ponder the tribulations of Boris Godunov.

•

By way of summary, it is to be observed that the geographic-national groups which have exerted the greatest influence upon the development of choral literature have been the French, the Italian, the Flemish, the German, the English, and the Russian. The particular effect of differing national conceptions is to be especially noted by the choral conductor with respect to: *(a)* manner of the rhythmic treatment, *(b)* character of the melodic-harmonic concept, *(c)* degree of emotional expressiveness.

CHAPTER X

THE INDIVIDUAL COMPOSER

The idea of "style," as pointed out above, represents a duality of concept, involving both the creative composer and the re-creative interpreter. Certain geographic and national influences have been discussed with relation to their effect as stylistic determinants. These influences may be regarded as more or less general in nature, since they cut across all periods and may apply to any number of persons widely separated in time or locality. Attention will now be turned to the composer as individual rather than as member of the group.

How may one recognize the writing of one person as being preeminently his own work and not that of another? What vocabulary has he employed for the expression of his ideas? What principles apply to the interpretation of his work that are peculiarly proper to its performance as contrasted with the performance of the works of others? Such questions recall elements mentioned earlier, namely, *(a)* the personality of the composer himself,*(b)* his technical equipment,*(c)* "the state of the grammar of the art," *(d)* his geographical and national group affiliation, *(e)* the historical and social background of the day.

a. The element of personality is obviously the most singularly individual of the stylistic determinants and furthest removed from the consideration of the man as a member of the group.

How is one to ascertain the specific personality? First acquaintance is usually furnished through contact with the music. Seldom does one become familiar with a composer's music without feeling something at least of the man's personality and temperament. The student who has studied, sung, and played Bach scores cannot fail to perceive something of the inner quality of the essential Bach. No one who has any knowledge at all of the music of Haydn can escape

102

catching from these scores something of the warmth and genial humanness of the man. The music of Beethoven reveals a man possessed with deep seriousness of purpose, the profundity of whose thought is relieved by frequent outbursts of simple gaiety. Gesualdo, Prince of Venosa, steps from his music as a man of intense emotional moods, passionate, daring and bold. Similarly with most of the masters: it is through the music that the first glimpse of the man is afforded.

Secondly, the conception revealed in the music should be illumined and widened through the study of available critical writings, which admittedly often must be accepted with reservations. Predispositions of the critic, personal prejudices and individual preferences often operating unconsciously may produce biased attitudes toward the person under discussion. The pressure of such influences makes it more than occasionally difficult for the critic to obtain a clear perspective on the subject of his dissertation. Consequently, while the student must read widely and lay hands on any and all material that may throw light upon the object of his research, he must weigh carefully what he finds, retaining for his own further use what seems pertinent and just, discarding what appears irrelevant or overly opinionated. Having first made a careful study of the composer's music and come to at least some recognition of the man himself, the student may draw on carefully evaluated critical estimates and analyses to amplify his knowledge, quicken his apperception of individual qualities and increase his depth of understanding.

b. The second determinant of the composer's style, his technical equipment, is also a property of the individual person rather than of the composer as member of the group. Technical equipment, like personality, is best discerned through experience with the actual music, not through the comment of others upon it, though the latter may sometimes help one to note fine points that might otherwise pass unobserved. By means of his own examination and analysis the student should decide for himself how thoroughly versed the particular composer may be in the technique of his craft, how adept in the weaving of contrapuntal fabric, how convincing with his harmonic progressions. The music should reveal what genius the composer has for the manipulation of rhythmic movement, how expert is his integration of the musical structure, with what clarity and distinctness he solves the problems of form and design. The student should determine for himself how skillful the composer may be in providing for instruments or voices material suitable to their powers of expression. It may be that the composer in question seeks particularly to develop an idiomatic language adapted to the capabilities of voices or instruments; it may be that he thinks of thematic material as musical material first and only secondarily as material intended for a specific medium. He may be of an experimental turn of mind, striving for an extension of the musical vocabulary; he may hear a new music which demands new methods of expression, new instruments, devices, and techniques.

Over and above all, the student should ascertain for himself the composer's capacity for endowing the score with life and meaning, for imparting that special quality without which the most correctly formed work exists as an inanimate shell.

For the conductor who strives for such an understanding, a sound musical training is prerequisite. The conductor must know music theory thoroughly, including harmony, the principles of contrapuntal writing, and the essentials of musical form. Only with this knowledge can he analyze the work with regard to its constituent elements and make an intelligent assay of its technical merit.

c. The third determinant of the composer's style, "the state of the grammar of the art," turns from a consideration of the composer as individual person toward his position as member of the group. The technical aspects of a composer's style are not formulated by his own technique alone; they are affected by the period in which the work is created. Successive epochs have a tendency to look upon the problem of art expression from entirely different points of view. There are ages whose technique seems firmly established and whose faith in traditional practice appears quietly serene; there are others that seem daemonically possessed to cast off the bonds of the old law and whose struggle to escape into a new era of expression captures the imagination by its very fierceness. Sensitivity of interpretation is only possible when there is an awareness of these varying attitudes and changing techniques.

Later chapters will take up the various historical periods of choral literature, which are also the great historical periods of music in general. Attention will be given to the technical ideals and aims of the various periods and to the matter of their application in choral music. For the present, suffice it to say that from age to age musical concepts vary with regard to harmonic relationships, the connections existing between rhythm and meter, preference for a prevailingly harmonic scheme over a preponderantly contrapuntal plan, and so on. The conductor who is to have a real understanding of "the state of the grammar of the art" of any given period must possess two-fold knowledge. In addition to competence in matters of music theory he must have knowledge of the historical developments in art; he must be aware of the technical considerations motivating the musical artists of any particular day.

d. The fourth determinant, geographical and national group affiliation, has been previously discussed — briefly with respect to the influence of language upon the musical rhetoric, and more extensively later in consideration of the formulation of style.

e. The fifth factor, that of the historical and social background, may be said to represent the climax of this study. As far as the present-day choral conductor is concerned, it is the determinant with which he is usually least acquainted and it is paradoxically the one that he should know best. The common procedure of beginning the study of choral literature with a series of individual pieces and through them arriving at a possibly dim picture of the creat-

ive personality, progressing from there somewhat haphazard-
ly to a hazy comprehension of the technical aspects of the
work of a given people or period, should be reversed. The
study of choral literature which has any serious intent should
properly begin with a survey of the great historic periods.
It has been said above that for full appreciation of the music
one must have some knowledge of the man who has written
it; to know the man one must know the scene from which he
has emerged.

The work of art is not an esoteric, mysterious thing suddenly and inexplicably bursting forth full-flowered. Its growth follows a logical process, conditioned by the society in
which it is produced. Although it partakes of the mysterious
and the sublime — otherwise it would not be art at all but
only craft — it is nevertheless created out of its own day
and proceeds from it.

Just as technique varies from age to age, so also do
more generalized esthetic standards, conforming to changing
conditions of different cultures. What the artist of one age
considers a fit subject for artistic expression may be rejected
by the artist of another time as totally unsuited to artistic
treatment. What is beautiful to the artist of one era may be
considered by the artist of another era to be completely lacking in requisite qualities. As McKinney and Anderson put it:

> Art, even considered in the most abstract way, is the
> result of the desire of the artist to create something
> that will satisfy himself through the manipulation of
> certain arrangements of shape, size, mass, time, and
> so forth — what the aestheticians call *beauty*. And
> all the arts, especially music, have tended to express
> the sense of beauty in certain periods according to
> definite ideals. Which means that the conception of
> beauty has been a constantly changing idea during
> the ages, one which has altered itself to suit the
> ideals of the historical period during which it was
> produced. It means also that in order to appreciate
> the manifestations of a work of art, we should know

the general life and thought of the period which brought it into being and how the sonata, the sonnet, the cathedral, the painting, reflecting this life and thought, are related to the other intellectual products of the time.

. . . .

None of the arts — and this is especially true of music — has developed in a void, unassociated with its time and period . . . . To understand music as we have it today, it is necessary to know something of the forces which have shaped and conditioned the various epochs of its growth. Music reflects the temper of the time that gives it birth and has a definite relationship to the political, economic, and cultural conditions that surround its composers and practitioners.[11]

All of which points to the necessity of complete immersion in the period during which a work has been produced in order that the interpreter may be able to re-create it properly. One obviously should be sympathetic with and have a feeling for the work at hand as an individual item. But, for complete mastery one also must see it in reference to the age during which it was brought into being and must have some knowledge at least of the conditions of its original creation.

The quality of the art of any day is affected by all the diverse strands which go to make up its cultural pattern: by the philosophy and thought-attitude of the day, by economic conditions, by the relationship existing between government and people, by the strength of the social ideal as a motive in the life of the times or by its failure as an effective force. The art-form is conditioned by the language of the people and by the tone of expression, by social habits and conventions. Hugo Leichtentritt in his illuminating and pro-

---

11 *Music in History*, New York, American Book Co., 1940, pp. 6, vi.

vocative work *Music, History, and Ideas* [12] discusses at length the factors within the particular era which affect its own formation and that of its art.

The interpreter must orient himself to the age in order to achieve the insight necessary for re-creating its thought. The work of art is endowed with qualities of mind and feeling which perhaps do not lie immediately on the surface but still yield themselves to the person who has the knowledge and the sensitivity to detect their presence. The fact that the work of art possesses a hidden, inner meaning which does not give itself up to the chance passerby is indicated by Helen Parkhurst when she says in speaking of the cathedral as an art-form, "Only so much of the rich content will be revealed to us as we ourselves can match from our store of memories." [13] The author goes on to note that the appreciation of the cathedral as an art-form is conditioned by the extent of the spectator's acquaintance with it as an architectural creation. The appreciation of *one* cathedral is made complete only by the experience of having beheld *many* cathedrals. This may be paraphrased to say that for delight in *one* madrigal one should have had experience with *many* madrigals. For enjoying one example of Baroque music one must have known many examples of Baroque music. In other words, the extent and breadth of appreciation is conditioned by the extent and breadth of experience.

Granted that no man can attain complete mastery of all the fields of human endeavor, the interpreter must nevertheless strive to obtain some idea of the general character of the culture of a given day and of the characteristic tone of its art expression. He must also develop enough sympathy for the attitude of the time to re-create its thought with sensitivity and understanding. The conductor should be thoroughly informed concerning the characteristics of the periods

---

12 Cambridge, Mass., Harvard University Press, 8th Printing, 1947, cop. 1938.

13 *Cathedral: A Gothic Pilgrimage*, Boston, Houghton, Mifflin, 1936, p. 257.

listed at the beginning of Chapter IX. In the following chapters these periods will be taken up in order, with consideration of the principles that are fundamental in the interpretation
of typical works of each period.

CHAPTER XI

THE RENAISSANCE
1425-1600

As each historic period is investigated in these chapters, the treatment proper to the choral work of the era in question will be described with reference to the following points:

a. Meter and tempo.

b. Structural relationship between counterpoint and harmony.

c. Expressive quality of the score.

d. Dynamic scheme.

These would seem to constitute the factors most susceptible to variation during the several periods. They also represent elements which the conductor can grasp as more or less apprehensible and for that reason are capable of being manipulated so that a logical and musically satisfying performance may be achieved.

As indicated earlier, no attempt is made to circumscribe the limits of any era categorically. The passage from one period to the next often represents a process of slow transformation, rather than of abrupt metamorphosis. Transitional periods partake of the characteristics of the eras that precede and follow, belonging wholly neither to the one nor to the other. However, for convenience in study a classification is adopted that indicates an approximate definition of periods during which certain general tendencies are observable.

In addition to the impossibility of setting fixed limits for particular cultural eras, the period approach entails a further difficulty: that of settling upon any conclusion which will encompass all the trends in any field of life or art during a given period. The expressional form of any art takes a number of diverse paths in any culture. Not only do the conceptions of the artist vary from age to age; they also vary

110

within the age. No single principle constitutes the motivating force for all the artists of any period. However, the present purpose is to obtain an over-all view of the field. In surveying the art of any given time it will be manifest that, although diverse tendencies are observable, still it is possible to discern certain basic trends which seem to be dominant.

The first period to which attention will be given here is the Renaissance, which may be said to comprise roughly the years 1425-1600. This era is found to be broken up into any number of separate movements. Various national groups appear from time to time, come to ascendancy and retreat to positions of lesser prominence. Various concepts concerning the nature and treatment of artistic expression arise, flourish, and wane. Nevertheless it is possible to formulate certain generalizations that will hold good for the interpretation of the music.

The first problem which faces the interpreter of Renaissance music is that of ascertaining the true meaning of the score. To quote from Manfred F. Bukofzer, "On the Performance of Renaissance Music":

> The performance of music becomes a problem only in modern music and in old music, that is to say, only when a traditional manner of performance not yet or no longer exists. In modern music the composer and the performers eventually establish a tradition of correct performance; the correct performance of old music must be reconstructed from primary and secondary sources, because the traditional manner of performance has been forgotten.[14]

It is this lack of knowledge concerning the performance traditions of the period that makes it so necessary for the interpreter to have some conception at least of the artistic principles of the age. Lacking a source of authority, he must

---

14 *MTNA Proceedings*, XXXVI (1941), 225.

deduce his own ideas of performance procedure through knowledge of the usages of the time.

As a matter of fact, no score, however accurate in notation and no matter how specific in the employment of directional terms, can indicate the exact performance intention of the composer. Those aspects which cannot be defined through notation and terminology the interpreter must reconstruct out of his knowledge of the conventions of the period and his feeling for the expressive quality of the art. The problem becomes more acute as one approaches those periods more remote in point of time from the present. All the more reason that the subjective reactions of the interpreter should be based on a sound knowledge of the esthetic creed and the technical principles of the period from which the work proceeds.

a. Meter and tempo. Renaissance ideas of rhythm differ widely from those of later musical practice. Today rhythm is often confounded with meter. Rhythmic pulsations have always existed as the backbone of the musical body, but it is possible for such pulsations to exist without being circumscribed by the regularly recurring patterns of the metrical concept.

Metrical organization is not necessarily a modern idea. It had been evident as early as the twelfth century in the rhythmic modes of the School of Notre Dame, whose leaders were Leonin and Perotin, the exact dates of their lives being now unknown. It was in the Baroque period, however, that meter assumed the particular type of dominance which it was to retain until modern times. To many persons the words "rhythm" and "meter" still are synonymous.

R. O. Morris describes the dualism in the Renaissance approach to rhythm and provides a more or less clear distinction between these two terms. Rhythmic contours were developed according to the declamation of the words so that:

> The *rhythmical* accentuation of each part is free, but, independently of the actual rhythmic accents, there is an imaginary *metrical* accentuation which imposes

a regular alternation of strong and weak beats to which the harmony of the composition has to conform, although the melody of each voice pursues its own way untrammelled.

He goes on to say:

. . . in the polyphonic music of the sixteenth century a double system of accentuation is employed. The rhythmical accentuation of each individual part is free, that is to say, the accents do not occur at strictly regular intervals, whereas the composition as a whole does conform to a fixed metrical scheme in which strong and weak accents succeed one another in a pre-determined order.

. . . .

Between the rhythmical accent (the accent of stress) and the metrical accent (the accent of quantity) there is a continual interplay; sometimes they coincide, sometimes they are at odds, and the rhythmical problem before the poet is to strike the just balance. Too much coincidence means monotony; too much at-oddness means chaos.[15]

Meter then does not automatically bring with it stress. During the Renaissance it has to do with the measuring out of the pulsations with reference to elapsed time. Accent has no inevitable connection with meter but refers to weight or stress applied at a particular point, that point being determined according to the relative importance of textual values. It would seem that the men of the Renaissance were able to make a clear demarcation in their minds between these two aspects of rhythm, whereas for the most part common practice from the Baroque period down to the present has tended to merge them.

The bar-line appeared as a notational sign in choral

15 *Contrapuntal Technique in the Sixteenth Century*, Oxford, Clarendon Press, 1922, pp. 3-4, 17, 18.

music during the late Renaissance with a function entirely
different from that which it fulfills according to the modern
idea. At the time of its origin it was merely a vertical line
intended to act as a quantitative gauge of elapsed time and
to serve as a convenience in keeping the various parts together. There was no relation implied between the bar-line
and a stressed accent, the latter being determined largely
by word values. The bar-line occurring in current editions
is a device added by editors in conformity with modern practice. There are those who advocate that the so-called "early"
works be published without any such lines. Publishers who
favor this procedure indicate metrical grouping by various
notational devices, but without the heavy vertical mark of
the bar-line which seems to carry an inescapable psychological impulse toward a stress accent.

Musical rhythm in Renaissance music stems from word-
rhythm. For the interpreter of Renaissance choral music this
means that metrical accent as such is to be avoided. Proper
interpretation demands that the accentual scheme result
from emphasizing important words to the degree warranted
by their relative value to the thought. The conductor will
delineate the rhythmic pulsation (the beat) with firmness in
order to synchronize the parts. At the same time he will
avoid the regular metrical accentuation common to the musical practice of a later date. There must be a sense of
grace and of ease in the progression from accent to accent,
continuity of movement and fluidity of pulse being vital to
the performance of this literature.

Considerable flexibility is observed in the matter of
tempo. The basic tempo is determined by the emotional or
dramatic mood of the text, that tempo being in general maintained for the duration of a work or a section thereof. Alterations of tempo are made in accordance with changes in the
textual mood. Such alterations ordinarily occur between sections, where a new thought in the text serves to introduce
a corresponding change in musical texture. Within the section
itself tempo variations are to be employed sparingly, and

usually with such subtlety and gradualness that the exact
point of the alteration of the pace is not perceptible to the
listener. Too much change of tempo in the course of the
work destroys the symmetry and proportion which constitute
the essence of Renaissance art. The article on "Rhythm"
in the *Harvard Dictionary of Music* will prove of value in
connection with this problem. Material dealing with early
rhythmic concepts will be found in *Music in the Middle Ages*
by Gustave Reese, Chapters VII, VIII, X, XI, and XII.[16]

  b. Structural relationship between counterpoint and harmony. The Renaissance concept of texture is a predominantly contrapuntal one, music of the period often being described as horizontal in its implications. The structure of the
great majority of the works depends upon a combination of
elements interlocked through the cohesive effect of independent and yet closely related contrapuntal constituents.

By the time of Dufay and his contemporaries in the early
fifteenth century the use of imitation had begun to emerge
as a factor in the structural aspect of the musical work. It
gradually gained in significance and persisted as an integral
element throughout the Late Renaissance, and has continued
down to the present as a contrapuntal device. As a conspicuous characteristic of the sixteenth-century motet and madrigal, it deserves particular attention from performers of
Renaissance music.

The term "point of imitation" indicates a passage in
which a figure or motive is given out by one voice and taken
up in imitative fashion by other voices successively. The
interpreter of contrapuntal music must handle the various
strands of the musical fabric so that the points of imitation
are heard, but not so emphasized as to stand out unduly from
the texture. The principle may be adopted that as long as
the imitation is continued the voice which is stating the
subject should be emphasized slightly. At the point where
the imitation leaves off, the emphasis may be dropped and

---

16 New York, W. W. Norton, 1940.

the voice involved retreat to a more inconspicuous position. The imitating voice should not become so prominent as to distort the musical structure. The point of imitation is, in a way, a detail of musical architecture. It should make its contribution of interest to the design, but never take precedence over the unity of the whole. Quoting Charles Kennedy Scott, from his work entitled *Madrigal Singing:*

> In the performance of his part the Madrigal singer has scarcely ever to consider any other part, or to regulate the expression of his part, *in order that some other part may be shown up* . . . In expressing his part well he has sometimes to assert himself a little more than the others, but the others never have to give way to him. When he seems to yield, it is only because his part gives him no opportunity for making it prominent.[17]

The implication is that if a part is interesting it should be emphasized slightly; if uninteresting as melodic design, it should be allowed to recede into the background. As successive entries of imitating voices occur, the effect should be cumulative through the piling up of contrapuntal lines, each of which is on a parity with the others. There should be no sense of the entry of a principal voice to which other voices are to be subordinate.

The Renaissance choral fabric consists of the combination of lines which are each free and yet mutually related in such a way that they are not only independent but also interdependent. The singer of Renaissance music must have the ability to execute his part with complete freedom and independence. Yet, while maintaining his independence, he must weave his melodic line into a web shared by the other parts.

Harmony is not absent from the Renaissance score, but is present as a result of the contrapuntal workings. Hence the terms "coincidental" or "resultant" harmony mentioned

---

17 London, Oxford University Press, 2nd edition, 1931, p. 7.

earlier. The appearance of block-like contrasts of harmonic
material in the works of such masters as Marenzio, Gesualdo,
and even Palestrina is taken by some writers to prefigure
the strong harmonic predilections of seventeenth-century
Baroque texture.

   c. *Expressive quality of the score.* Close expressive
affinity of text and music is found in the Renaissance score.
The manner of dramatic and emotional expression in the
Renaissance is determined largely by the meaning of the
words. The representative choral music of the period is of
two types: *(a)* sacred music, the characteristic forms being
the mass and the motet, *(b)* secular music, the characteristic
forms being the madrigal and related types such as the
French chanson. The sacred music inclines toward a minimum of dramatic exploitation. The mass and the motet both
are forms particularly designed for the expression of univer-
salized religious emotion. They are impersonal rather than
personal in character, objective rather than subjective in
approach. Meditation and contemplation are the keynotes of
this religious life. Prayer is the characteristic attitude of
its worshippers. Therefore, there is in this music everything
conducive to the atmosphere of quiet reflection, little to
destroy the calm serenity of the devout soul.

   While the dramatic element of the mass and the motet
is to be minimized, it still is not to be ignored. The physical
aspect of the religious expression is not to be emphasized,
but it must not be denied. Consequently these forms should
be endowed with vitality. Although the choral director must
conduct the music of the Renaissance with restraint in expression, he must not confuse restraint with repression.
While Renaissance music — particularly the ecclesiastical
music — is discreet in the expression of human emotion, it
nevertheless must be re-created with sincerity of feeling
and firmness of purpose. Usually the most appropriate treatment is a quiet but sincere statement of the emotional implications of the text, leaning neither to theatrical exaggeration
nor to dullness.

Misunderstanding of the religious mysticism of the Renaissance has resulted in performances of the ecclesiastical music of the period as though it were a totally inanimate, lifeless thing. This music must never be allowed to become colorless and vapid; it must always have breath and spirit. It is imbued with warm religious fervor and deep sincerity of feeling; it must be performed with enthusiasm in its more vigorous utterances and with deep devotion in its quieter phases.

While the sacred music of the Renaissance is not lacking in drama, it is the drama of a universal mystical adoration, not the conflict of violent personal struggle. The men of the Renaissance found great joy in their religion; they experienced the sorrows of the tragic events of the life of Christ with the utmost sincerity of soul; but their joy was the joy of serenity, not of hilarity, their sorrow the sorrow of poignant grief rather than that of overwhelming melancholy.

The music of the madrigal and the chanson is less restrained than the music of the church in the expression of personal emotion. At the same time, it never reaches the point of abandon. There is a subtlety and elegance in the tonal language of these forms that usually keeps the manner of expression within certain bounds, seldom allowing it to go beyond the limits of "good taste." The composer of the Renaissance madrigal shows great concern for the expressive quality of the words. The underlying mood of the text establishes the character of the corresponding musical material. Much use is made of the devices of word painting. Particular phrases and individual words that possess a definitely pictorial character appeal strongly to the madrigal writers. The texts are searched for possibilities of picturesque coloristic and descriptive effects. Prunières expresses the matter aptly when he says of the madrigal:

> . . . the poetic text is its *raison d'être*, and the music
> reflects all the suggestions of that text. The compo-
> ser does not aim only at transposing into appropriate

melody and harmony the prevailing atmosphere of the short poem; he endeavours to paraphrase minutely its ideas and its very language. Long festoons of thirds weave themselves about the "chains of love"; sighs are translated by pauses and breaks in the melody; the idea of duration, of immobility, is expressed by the holding of a single voice, the others carrying on their parts relentlessly. The voices rise on the words "heaven," "heights," "ascension"; they fall on the words "earth," "sea," "abyss," "hell." The notes scatter in silvery groups round the words "laughter," "joyous," "gay." Finally "martyrdom," "sadness," "pain," "cruelty," "tears" are expressed by audacious discords and unexpected modulations.[18]

Thomas Morley writing in 1597 in his *Plaine and Easie Introduction to Practicall Musicke* indicates that the Elizabethans accepted personal expressiveness as a necessary quality of music when he says:

> . . . the parts of a *Madrigal* either of five or sixe parts go somtimes full, sometimes very single, sometimes jumping together, and somtime quite contrarie waies [wise], like unto the passion which they expresse, for as you schollers say that love is ful of hopes and feares, so is the Madrigall or lovers musicke full of diversitie of passions and ayres.
>
> . . . .
>
> It followeth to shew you how to dispose your musicke according to the nature of the words which you are therein to expresse, as whatsoever matter it be which you have in hand, such a kind of musicke must you frame to it. You must therefore if you have a grave matter, applie a grave kinde of musicke to it · if a merrie subject you must make your musicke also merrie. For it will be a great absurditie to use a sad

18 *Monteverdi: His Life and Work*, transl. from the French by Marie D. Mackie, London and Toronto, J. M. Dent, 1926, pp. 28-29.

harmonie to a merrie matter, or a merrie harmonie to
a sad lamentable or tragicall dittie [text].

. . . .

Also, if the subject be light, you must cause your
musicke go in motions, which carrie with them a
celeritie or quicknesse of time, as minimes, crotchets
and quavers: if it be lamentable, the note must goe
in slow and heavie motions, as semi-breves, breves
and such like, . . . Moreover, you must have a care
that when your matter signifieth ascending, high
heaven, and such like, you make your musicke ascend: and by the contrarie where your dittie speaketh
of descending lowenes, depth, hell, and others such,
you must make your musicke descend, for as it will
be thought a great absurditie to talke of heaven and
point downwarde to the earth: so will it be counted
great incongruitie if a musician upon the wordes hee
ascended into heaven shoulde cause his musicke
descend, or by the contrarie upon the descension
should cause his musicke to ascend.

In speaking of the motet, Morley goes on to say:

This kind of al others which are made on a ditty,
requireth most art, and moveth and causeth most
strange effects in the hearer, being aptlie framed for
the dittie and well expressed by the singer, for it
will draw the auditor (and speciallie the skilfull auditor) into a devout and reverent kind of consideration
of him for whose praise it was made.

Morley indicates that the expression of feeling lies not only
in the province of the composer but also in the domain of the
performer:

But I see not what passions or motions it can stirre
up, being sung as most men doe commonlie sing it:
that is, leaving out the dittie and singing onely the
bare note, as it were a musicke made onelie for in-

struments, which will in deed shew the nature of the
musicke, but never carrie the spirit and (as it were)
that livelie soule which the dittie giveth, but of this
enough. And to returne to the expressing of the ditty,
the matter is now come to that state that though a
song be never so wel made & never so aptlie applied
to the words, yet shal you hardlie find singers to
expresse it as it ought to be, for most of our church
men, (so they can crie louder in ye quier [choir] than
their fellowes) care for no more, whereas by the contrarie, they ought to studie howe to vowell and sing
cleane, expressing their wordes with devotion and
passion, whereby to draw the hearer as it were in
chaines of gold by the eares to the consideration of
holie things.

Morley turns from the motet to the madrigal, of which he says:

. . . it is next unto the Motet, the most artificiall
[artfully contrived] and to men of understanding most
delightfull. If therefore you will compose in this kind
you must possesse your selfe with an amorus humor
(for in no composition shal you prove admirable except you put on, and possesse your selfe wholy with
that vaine wherein you compose) so that you must in
your musicke be wavering like the wind, sometime
wanton, somtime drooping, sometime grave and staide,
otherwhile effeminat, you may maintaine points and
revert them, use triplaes and shew the verie utter-
most of your varietie, and the more varietie you shew
the better shal you please.[19]

Surely the man who wrote thus of the music of the English
Renaissance could never imagine music as unemotional or
personally unexpressive. The difference between the expressiveness of Morley's day and of ours is a difference in
the degree of the intensity of the statement and in the means

19 London, Peter Short, 1597, pp. 172, 177-180.

of expression, not a difference between absence and presence of feeling. Morley's dicta are clear regarding the composer's duty to write so that the music may express the true meaning of the word, and concerning the performer's responsibility to re-create for the listener the ideas and emotions inherent in the text. These statements of one of the acknowledged masters of the Renaissance should dispel an all too prevalent tendency to perform Renaissance music with such lack of dramatic feeling that it becomes anemic or with such delicacy that it becomes precious. Emotional implications should be carried out with an emphasis that is firm though restrained and with an avoidance of any exaggeration that would disturb the poise and balance of the word. Scott has this to say of the expressive quality of the madrigal:

> Madrigal music will take us through moods ranging from simple gaiety to profound reflection. But it will neither give us the storm and stress of objective nature, nor even of human nature. It never runs loose. It is sincere, with the ardency of new adventure. But its sincerity is tempered with a certain emotional restrained, inherent in the polyphonic style itself, . . .[20]

d. Dynamic scheme. Like expressive quality, dynamic design is closely related to textual considerations, being more or less implicit in the word values. The so-called madrigal- or motet-form is conditioned by the thought structure of the text, each section of which is usually provided with a corresponding section of music. A change in the thought customarily brings a change in musical material. As a general rule the form is of a sectional type, in which the musical structure is set up by assigning a new point of imitation to the beginning of each new section of the text.

The general dynamic treatment for each section depends upon the quality of the basic thought of that section. Dynamic contrast is often employed to bring out the change in thought in proceeding from one section to the next. As is the case

---

[20] *Madrigal Singing*, p. 4.

with tempo modification, changes in dynamics are moderate, the ranges from upper to lower levels being less extreme than in the music of later eras. While changes from section to section are occasionally accompanied by the comparatively sudden adoption of new levels, still the degree of difference in actual dynamic intensity is usually relatively modest.

The abruptness of any sudden change is often reduced by overlapping in the contrapuntal structure. A new section, with a corresponding change of dynamic intensity, is often introduced in one part while the others are concluding the previous section. Thus dynamic changes are rendered less obvious than when all parts start a new section simultaneously.

There has been a widespread misconception that polyphonic music lacks dynamic variety. This misconception is due partly to the structural devices just cited. It is also due to lack of awareness of the close relationship between dynamics and text. Dynamic variation proceeds according to the phrase contour, corresponding to the thought content. As with tempo modification, such changes are accomplished gradually. The swelling and the diminishing of tone are of a subtle character, achieved so gradually that the listener ordinarily is hardly aware that a change is in process. The long crescendo as such does not appear until the eighteenth century and is not properly employed in Renaissance music.

Since the curve of the dynamic line is the result of the intensification of the key words in the phrase, the very nature of the contrapuntal style produces a combination of dynamic curves whose high and low points do not coincide. The fact that often in contrapuntal writing the various participating voices do not have the same word at the same time makes the synchronization of the curves an impossibility. Therein lies a great part of the charm of polyphonic writing, the "continual give-and-take" which J. A. Fuller Maitland indicates as an essential element of the polyphonic style.[21]

21 *The Consort of Music: A Study of Interpretation and Ensemble,* Oxford, Clarendon Press, 1915, p. 152.

In summing up the attributes of Renaissance music with reference to their implications for the interpretation of choral literature, the first point to recall is the close alliance between text and music. The whole substance of Renaissance vocal music takes its shape from the motivating force of the text. Rhythm, expressive representation, dynamic treatment, all are given their characteristic form through the operation upon the composer's imagination of the word as stimulus. It is imperative, therefore, that the interpreter devote his first attention to a careful study of the text and the relationships between it and the musical structure.

Secondly, the conductor must be aware that the phraseology of the Renaissance choral work is determined by the contrapuntal idiom. He must realize that the Renaissance style is pre-eminently a polyphonic one, whose concept is that of a series of lines proceeding in a horizontal direction, whose implications, first of all, are individually melodic and only secondarily harmonic.

Lastly, he must realize that the musical statement of the Renaissance is usually set forth with decorum and dignity, that, while it is human and alive, awake to all the shades of emotional expression, gay and somber alike, it is at the same time controlled in its manner of utterance. Normally restrained in tone, avoiding the extremes of expression, it speaks with moderation and poise.

CHAPTER XII

THE BAROQUE ERA
1600-1750

The term "Baroque" has been employed by historians of art, literature, and music to identify the cultural trends of the seventeenth and early eighteenth centuries. The Venetian school, which came to a climax with Giovanni Gabrieli, 1557-1612, gives evidence of the beginning of Baroque style in music. The passing of Bach and Handel, in 1750 and 1759 respectively, may be said to mark the close of the period.

The Baroque is an era of great contrasts, both spiritual and secular. Physical love of life is combined with the exaltation of religious emotion. Religious rapture is contrasted with the agonies of martyrdom. Love of power and magnificence are everywhere evident. Spaciousness and richness are qualities greatly admired and sought in all the art expressions of the time. Emphasis is placed on size and impressiveness. Tremendous areas are inclosed by architects in designing the buildings of the day. Rich decoration is applied to increase the stately effect. Dynamism, the love of motion, is observable as an impelling factor in artistic creation. Soaring lines, ebullient swellings and convolutions, expansive, rolling curves characterize the music, the architecture, the paintings, the literature. Everywhere there is visible the piling up of theatrical and dramatic effect, the use of strong color areas, alternations of light and shade, violent contrasts of emotional representation.

Secularism grows in all departments of life. The church, which had been the controlling element of society through the medieval period, saw its authority shaken in the Renaissance, and during the Baroque Era yields place to the state as the source of temporal authority. Reluctant to surrender position and prestige, the church makes a new appeal through the glorious pageantry of the Counter-Reformation.

With the waning of ecclesiastical power and the ascend-

125

ance of the state, the importance of princes and hereditary sovereigns increases. Magnificent palaces are built, fitting the status of powerful rulers. Splendid furniture is designed and fine paintings are produced to equip these sumptuous dwellings. Poets lend their efforts to extolling the virtues of the ruler and to beguile his thoughts in leisure moments. Musicians practice their art to entertain the nobleman and his guests and to provide a pleasant pastime. Everywhere art is pressed into service: to glorify the ruler, to add to the pomp and brilliance of the Counter-Reformation, to amuse, to entertain, to contribute to the lustrous panorama of life, be it the worldly spectacle of the temporal ruler or the religious magnificence of the church. Baroque music reflects the characteristics of the Baroque habit of thought and expression. Impressive, dynamic movement, rich effects of harmonic color, dignity of utterance, above all, intensified emotional expression — these are components of the best Baroque music.

The year 1600 marks the beginning of a new musical era. A group of persons known as the Florentine Camerata provided the impetus for changing conceptions in music at that time. The artistic creed was codified by Giulio Caccini, c. 1546-1618, who in the preface to a publication entitled *Le Nuove Musiche* (literally, *The New Musics*), 1602, gave expression to the new spirit of the day. The title of the work, *Nuove Musiche*, was adopted to designate the new style, differentiating it from that of the preceding era.

The aim of the Camerata was to return to what was thought to be the ideal of the old Greek drama with its insistence on the dramatic purport of the text and on communicating the essence of the story to the audience. Emphasis was placed on clear projection of words. Singing assumed a declamatory character as most suitable for conveying the word-idea. The term *stile recitativo* indicates the new style of singing arising from concentration upon textual declamation. This reanimation of the Greek dramatic ideal led to the development of the opera. Some authorities see the beginnings of opera in the so-called madrigal comedies or "madrigal operas" of the Late Renaissance, where dramatic continuity was derived from a story sung, but not acted, in a series of related madrigals.

In the field of sacred music, oratorio appeared as the counterpart of the opera. At first there was little difference between the two forms, the early oratorios being to all intents and purposes merely operas upon sacred themes. Other choral forms cultivated in the Baroque Era were the passion, the cantata, the mass, the motet, and the chorale. The passion is akin to the oratorio. Its distinguishing characteristic lies in its theme, which deals with the events of the last days of Christ on earth. Plainsong settings of the passion had been employed since the Middle Ages and many polyphonic settings were written during the Renaissance, but the form came into particular favor during the Baroque period.

The term cantata has been applied somewhat indiscriminately to a number of widely varying forms. The church cantata may be described as a diminutive oratorio. The secular cantata is similar in construction, but employs a secular text. The mass and the motet decline in artistic significance but are still written during this period and, as a matter of fact, are produced throughout all the course of history to serve the purposes of the worship for which they are intended. The seventeenth- and eighteenth-century mass and motet show the impact of the growing secular and operatic influences of the Baroque and reveal a modification in style owing to the changing concepts of the day. The chorale had come into great prominence during the Reformation period of Martin Luther, 1483-1546, although its early history far antedates his time. It continues through the seventeenth and eighteenth centuries as a typically Germanic choral form.

a. Meter and tempo. With the seventeenth century the musical score takes on a more definitely metrical character. The accentuations are placed at regularly spaced intervals rather than, as previously, at irregularly spaced intervals according to the word values. The bar-line now marks an accent. At the same time, the coexistence of the metrical concept and the declamatory idea produces two types of solo song: *(a) recitative*, which is ametrical in character, taking its cue from the prose rhythms of the text, and *(b) aria*, which is inclined toward metrical organization, depending upon purely musical-rhythmic requirements rather than upon word values. A third type, *arioso*, lies midway between recitative and aria in style, possessing something of the character of each.

The conductor of Baroque music will employ a more vigorous accentuation of the beat than is used with Renaissance literature. He customarily will employ a comparatively regular metrical patterning, giving to the first beat of each measure a reasonably decisive accent, though avoiding exaggeration. Recitative passages will be conducted in a freer rhythmic pulse with no sense of set metrical patterns. In recitative the successions of beats will allow the singer to declaim the words somewhat as though he were reciting them upon the indicated pitches.

Baroque music, in accordance with the temper of the age, moves with a certain sense of dignity and impressiveness. The massiveness of the Baroque esthetic formula is mirrored in the weight and resolute firmness of the rhythmic step. The period is inclined toward a constancy of rhythmic movement and a deliberateness of pace. Tempos are in the main moderate. Even in a rapid tempo, the sensation is of unhurried animation rather than of precipitate haste. The metrical pattern, having been once set up, continues in fairly unbroken succession for the duration of the work or section. Tempo rubato is employed according to implications of the text, but only with the greatest discretion. The use of tempo rubato is attested by Girolamo Frescobaldi, 1583-1643, in the preface to his *Toccate*, a part of which Arnold Dolmetsch quotes as follows:

I°. Firstly, that kind of style must not be subject to time. We see the same thing done in modern madrigals, which, notwithstanding their difficulties, are rendered easier to sing, thanks to the variations of the time, which is beaten now slowly, now quickly, and even held in the air, according to the expression of the music, or the sense of the words.[22]

It is apparent that this music is not to be treated as rhythmically inflexible. These works have the quality of freedom. But while they possess elasticity of pace and while ritardandos and accelerandos occur, such changes are infrequent in comparison with their prolific use by later composers. Further, the tempo rubato is treated with great subtlety so that the change in movement is accomplished with smoothness. As the Baroque period proceeds from its early to its later phases, the tempo rubato of the early seventeenth-century declamatory style tends to give way to a greater regularity. A more sparing use is made of the ritardando and an even more economical use of accelerando. One of the essential characteristics of the music of the High Baroque is its sense of strong rhythmic drive, of steady propulsion through time.

The ritardando in music of the High Baroque is more often applied at the conclusion of the section where it has the effect of a slight broadening designed to underline the cadential effect. Many choral conductors exaggerate the retard, and use it with much greater frequency than they should. The excessive and frequent slowing down of the tempo heard in much present-day choral performance is out of keeping with the Baroque concept of rhythmic movement where the idea is that of a reasonably regular progression from first note to last, with a slight retard here and there for broadening, but with comparatively undisturbed flow of the metrical pulse.

b. Structural relationship between counterpoint and harmony. One of the strongest tendencies of the new music is a reaction against the previously prevailing contrapuntal meth-

---

22 *The Interpretation of the Music of the XVIIth and XVIIIth Centuries,* London, Novello, 1915, p. 5.

od. Increasing concern with the intricacies of contrapuntal technique and delight in the exploration and extension of contrapuntal elaborations had led to a degree of complexity against which the Camerata rebelled. The contrapuntal maze had often become so involved that the sense of the words was completely obscured by the movement of the parts. It was against the excesses of this style that the Camerata raised its voice. Monodic singing was the natural outcome of the revolt. As the early seventeenth century saw it, the medium for the expression of the word-idea was not to be a group of voices each spinning out its own version of the story, but, rather, one voice declaiming its part against an accompaniment provided either by other voices or by instruments.

A distinction, adopted by more recent writers, should be made here between the terms "monodic," which refers to music for solo voice and accompaniment, and "monophonic," which implies a single melodic line unaccompanied. "Monody" means accompanied solo song; "monophony" is properly reserved for unaccompanied unisonal music of the type of plainsong, in contrast with "polyphony." The term "homophonic" is often employed synonymously with the term "monodic" to indicate music for a principal melodic line plus accompanying parts, but there is a commendable tendency to use the former only where the main melody and the accompanying parts all move more or less together rhythmically, as in an ordinary harmonized hymn.

The composers of the seventeenth century turned away from the concept of a melody as related to and combined with other melodies, to a concept of one melody accompanied by harmonic support. Furthermore, harmony shows evidence of becoming a separate consideration, an end sought in itself.

From the concept of a melody supported by harmonic background arose the principle of the *basso continuo* or thorough bass. *Basso continuo* technique consists in providing the melodic lines for the principal parts, vocal or instrumental, with a fundamental bass part as support. The bass part, which is written out, is accompanied by a series of numerals and symbols indicating the harmonic background to be supplied. The details of voice leading are left to the discretion of the performer. Skill in improvising was expected of the seventeenth-century musician. *Basso continuo* or thorough bass practice became so universal in the Baroque Era that music historians sometimes refer to it as the "thorough bass period."

So complete was the dominance of the melodic-harmonic concept that the contrapuntal style momentarily all but vanished from the scene. Polyphony for a time was almost totally obliterated in the vocal music of Italy and France. It lingered, however, in the writings of the North Europeans, notably in the compositions of Johann Hermann Schein, 1586-1630, Samuel Scheidt, 1587-1654, and Heinrich Schütz, 1585-1672, and it came to full flower with Johann Sebastian Bach, 1685-1750.

The improvisatory aspect of the style made it possible for the performer to add all manner of decorative figures of his own invention. To a considerable extent his excellence was judged according to the measure of his skill in contriving elaborate figuration and decorative devices. So widespread was the use of ornamentation that a veritable science evolved concerning musical ornaments. Rooted in Renaissance practice and theory, this science was further developed in treatises of the Baroque and later, and still serves as the object of musicological research. This love of musical elaboration is a truly Baroque phenomenon. It is the expression in music of a trait which has been noted previously as running through all phases of the Baroque mentality — the love of the ornate, the predilection for movement such as the ornamental line provides. Abuse of the system of ornamentation led to the artificial operatic music of the late seventeenth century. Over-adulation of improvisatory skill in singing prompted the extravagances of the virtuoso school of operatic singing.

Counterpoint did not completely disappear even in the

south, and following its momentary eclipse reasserted itself as an important factor in the determination of texture. It was employed particularly by the Italian violin composers: Giovanni Battista Vitali, c. 1644-1692; Arcangelo Corelli, 1653-1713; Felice dall'Abaco, 1675-1742; Francesco Geminiani, 1687-1762. In choral music counterpoint pervades the work of Giovanni Legrenzi, 1626-1690, Carlo Pallavicini, 1630-1688, Alessandro Stradella, c. 1645-1682, and Vitali. A significant contrapuntal technique was developed by the Viennese master Johann Joseph Fux, 1660-1741, whose treatise *Gradus ad Parnassum*, 1725, is still today a source of information regarding the principles of strict counterpoint. Antonio Caldara, 1670-1736, combined contrapuntal dexterity with the innately Italian gift for a smooth, expressive melodic contour.

The harmonic implications of Baroque counterpoint are in general stronger than are those of Renaissance counterpoint. As a matter of fact, in the Baroque period music takes on a predominantly harmonic aspect, with the result that harmonic requirements thereafter to some extent govern melodic development, rhythmic movement, and contrapuntal structure.

c. *Expressive quality of the score.* With the dawn of the Baroque period there comes a new emphasis on dramatic expressiveness. Once again the quality of the expression is determined by the word. The latter part of the sixteenth century had seen a growing interest in the emotional implication of the word as stimulus to musical creation. The early part of the seventeenth century witnesses a further intensification of the emotional aspect of the word-idea. Musical structure yields place to the representation of emotional conflict. There is consequently at the opening of the Baroque Era less striving for purely formal beauty than for dramatic effect. Consequently the interpreter must explore each word of the text as a possible means of conveying dramatic feeling.

Whereas the Renaissance had tended to occupy itself with the picturesque and descriptive quality of the word,

Baroque musicians tend to look for its emotional and theatrically dramatic possibilities. Where the Renaissance had made its emotional declaration with comparative reticence, the Baroque composer releases his tale with a sense of emotional outpouring. Still, the story possesses a quality of the impersonal; it does not evince the subjectivity of the romanticist. The emotion springs from tumultuous influences; it concerns itself with the conflict of great dramatic forces rather than with the struggle of human personalities. The dramatic personage of Baroque music is a type, a universal and eternal character, a representative of the whole human race; his experiences are universal experiences, common to all mankind rather than the individualized sufferings of a single hero.

During the latter part of the seventeenth century, growing preoccupation with beauty of form lightens the somewhat heavy statement of the emotional content which had appeared in the early Baroque. The emotional speech becomes less melodramatic in tone and is more quietly phrased; reticence now characterizes the emotional language.

Dissonance plays an increasingly important part in the representation of emotional mood. Not unknown during the Renaissance as a means of creating dramatic feeling, its use is now greatly widened. Chromaticism had been utilized by Luca Marenzio, *c.* 1560-1599, for the depiction of emotion. Great strides in this direction were made by Carlo Gesualdo, *c.* 1560-1613, whose striking and extraordinary use of dissonance and chromaticism approached a limit of intensity and of dramatic power up to that time unknown in music. It was Claudio Monteverdi, 1567-1643, however, who made the most significant contribution to the practice. Monteverdi is sometimes credited with the first employment of the unprepared dissonance, although this device had appeared sporadically before his time. In the main, however, dissonance had only been permissible when prepared, that is, only when the dissonant tone had first been heard as a consonance. It was Monteverdi who broke the restriction, making dissonance more readily available for expressive purposes.

It is apparent that the interpreter who would convey to the listener the dramatic implications of late Renaissance and early Baroque music must possess sound theoretical knowledge. If the clash of dissonance is to be re-created with the result intended by the composer, the interpreter must understand the relationship of the dissonance to the harmonic structure, and he must so treat the harmonic scheme that the real meaning of the dissonance comes forth.

The entire problem of the interpretation of seventeenth- and eighteenth-century music revolves around the *Affektenlehre* or "doctrine of affections," a term arising from Baroque concepts. The word "affection" in this context indicates what an English-speaking person more nearly comprehends as "emotion." The kernel of the *Affektenlehre* is the thesis that every work of art is characterized by a basic emotional tone, none existing in a wholly emotionless state. Furthermore, the basic affection is not to exist in the music alone but is to be awakened also within the listener.

The implication for the interpreter is that for the proper re-creation of the composer's intention the performer must himself comprehend the emotional statement he is to transmit to the hearer. The relation between music and listener is indicated by a quotation which Lang gives from a seventeenth-century treatise:

> Melancholy people like grave, solid, and sad harmony; sanguine persons prefer the *hyporchematic* style (dance music) because it agitates the blood; choleric people like agitated harmonies because of the vehemence of their swollen gall; martially inclined men are partial to trumpets and drums and reject all delicate and pure music; phlegmatic persons lean toward women's voices because their high-pitched voice has a benevolent effect on phlegmatic humour.[23]

The idea is a more involved one than that of the mere

---

23 Paul Henry Lang, *Music in Western Civilization*, New York, W. W. Norton, 1941, pp. 436-437.

communication of feeling. It implies the communication of certain specific feelings. It presupposes that an identical feeling will be awakened in each of the assembled listeners. For the communication of the specific feeling an extensive vocabulary is utilized. All the resources of the score are employed in such a way that the basic affection is set forth, clearly emphasized and high-lighted. Every element of the score constitutes a part of the vocabulary. Melodic contours, rhythmic organization, harmonic structure, the treatment of dissonance, orchestral and instrumental effects, all are to be so designed that the fundamental emotional and dramatic mood is transmuted into musical terms. It is assumed that certain rhythmic patterns possess definite affectional qualities; it is supposed that a particular melodic motive may carry a specific emotional connotation, that certain harmonic relationships provoke particular emotional states, and so with all the elements of the musical work.

d. *Dynamic scheme.* In her study *Origins of Musical Time and Expression* Rosamond Harding sets the earliest use of dynamic effects as such at about 1600.[24] Gustave Reese in *Music in the Renaissance* indicates a somewhat earlier date.[25] The first real dynamic device noted by scholars is that of the echo, the exact origin of which in musical practice has been widely debated. Whatever its early history, the relationship of the practical and the esthetic may be observed in the widespread use of the effect by the Venetians in the latter part of the Renaissance. The School of Venice was centered at the Cathedral of San Marco, which had as a feature of its interior design two separate choir lofts. It was a thoroughly natural thing for the master of the music at St. Mark's to station a group of performers in each gallery, employing them in antiphonal and echo fashion. Although the Venetians did not originate the practice of obtaining dynamic variety through antiphonal effect, Adrian Willaert, *c.* 1480-1562, one of the outstanding figures of the group, was the

---

[24] London, Oxford University Press, 1938, pp. 85-86.
[25] New York, W. W. Norton, 1954, p. 521.

first to employ the technique on a grand scale. Subsequent composers, notably Giovanni Gabrieli, 1557-1612, made wide use of the device, which through the universal popularity of the Venetian school was adopted by musicians in all parts of the then known world. Gabrieli's *Sonata Pian e Forte*, 1597, is an application in instrumental music of the echo principle. Sweelinck, 1562-1621, and Frescobaldi, 1583-1643, made wide use of it in organ music. Choral directors everywhere are familiar with the *Echo Song (O la, o che buon eccho)* by Lassus. *c.* 1530-1594. Cavalieri, *c.* 1550-1602, employed the echo effect in his oratorio *Rappresentazione di Anima et di Corpo*. The resulting contrast obtained by the alternation of forte and piano phrases became a characteristic feature of seventeenth- and eighteenth-century music.

The dynamic scheme of Baroque music is architectonic in character. It consists of the laying out of the dynamic colors in broad areas of massive proportion, with contrast obtained by the juxtaposition of extensive areas of differing dynamic values. In the main, there is little dynamic variation within the large area. Interest depends not upon variations of dynamics within the section but upon the contrast of the large masses.

In 1904 J. Vianna da Motta, writing in the *Neue Zeitschrift für Musik*,[26] employed the word "terrace" to indicate the architectonic character of Bach's music. He said:

> Dieser Musik ist immer mehr oder weniger Majestät zu eigen. Sie baut sich stetig auf in breiten Terrassen, wie die assyrischen Urtempel der Menschheit.

> (A certain majesty is always present to a greater or lesser degree in this music. It rises steadily in broad terraces, like those first early temples of mankind in Assyria.)

The term "terrace dynamics" has been employed by succeeding scholars to the Baroque concept of dynamic treat-

---

26 71. Jahrgang, No. 40., 28. September 1904. "Zur Pflege der Bachschen Klavierwerke," p. 679.

ment. The use of the dynamic terrace is a logical outcome of the previously discussed echo effect with its alternating forte and piano.

Since the long crescendo and diminuendo as dynamic devices do not become actually operative in choral literature until the late eighteenth century, the performer should not introduce them in Baroque music. The *messa di voce* of seventeenth-century practice is not actually a crescendo and decrescendo as those terms are understood today but rather an intensification of the word-idea. It is a dynamic effect executed as a result of emphasis on words whose basic *Affekt* is one of particular emotional and dramatic significance.

The Baroque style does not know the high and low levels of dynamic intensity which more recent periods have employed. Bach, for example, executes his dynamic pattern within the ranges from forte to piano for the most part. Only a very occasional fortissimo is encountered. For the greater part of the work a particular composition will very likely proceed through the middle level of the dynamic register, ranging up to forte and down to piano for purposes of dynamic coloration. Any further intensification in the direction of dynamic extremes is to be applied with caution.

Dynamic intensity in the Baroque Era is achieved largely by the piling up of successively entering contrapuntal lines. What is felt as growing dynamic power is often produced not through any change in the dynamic level but simply by the addition of more lines to the texture.

The matter of dynamics in the performance of Baroque literature is closely tied up with the sound ideal of the period. The term "sound ideal" means the tonal quality common to the musical practice of a certain composer or period. It proceeds principally from a consideration of timbre. It has a bearing upon size of performing body and, as far as the interpreter goes, should have a decided effect upon his control of dynamics. For instance, the sound ideal of the Renaissance is that of a group of voices performing together, probably *a cappella* or else accompanied by instruments whose lines in the main duplicate those of the voices. It is that of a comparatively small number of persons utilizing a preeminently vocal texture. The interpreter in working out the dynamic scheme for a particular work of the Renaissance must keep this sound ideal in mind, employing a scheme consistent with the characteristic timbres of such a group.

The sound ideal of the Baroque period is that of instruments and voices performing together. As it finds expression in the Bach accompanied choral works — which typify the style of the High Baroque — it presupposes a performance in which voices and instruments are of approximately equal weight. The instrumental body is conceived not as a subordinate, accompanying unit, but as made up of individuals whose part is equally important with that of the choral body. At the time of their creation these works were performed by a much smaller body of singers than is customarily employed today and utilized an approximately equivalent amount of instrumental tone. Charles S. Terry indicates a chorus of some seventeen voices with an orchestra of ten to twelve players as the number of performers usually available to Bach for their presentation.[27] Consequently, the choral conductor who is attempting to bring a Baroque work to life in the style of its period will do well not to try to marshal the tremendous chorus often employed at the present time. He should also decrease the gap which exists in much contemporary procedure between the size of the chorus and that of the orchestra. Choral body and instrumental ensemble should produce an approximately equivalent volume of tone.

The contemporary choral director often has a mistaken idea that he cannot perform the Bach works with anything less than a mammoth organization. Many choral groups of moderate or small size can give quite satisfactory performances of Baroque works. The full symphonic orchestra is not only not required but is usually a hindrance. It was not

---

27 *The Music of Bach,* London, Oxford University Press, 1933, p. 66.

a symphonic orchestra which was used in those days, but a more or less heterogeneous group of instruments, chosen in accordance with the resources available to the composer at the moment, or in line with the expressive necessities of the composition. The instrumentation of the Bach accompanied vocal works varies widely from score to score, and the choral conductor interested in re-creating these masterpieces in the style of their period can usually discover any number of them which are suitable for a small chorus and a few instrumentalists. The director interested in exploring the problem of the sound ideal and the performance practice of the Baroque period will find valuable assistance in the following works:

Manfred F. Bukofzer, *Music in the Baroque Era,* W. W. Norton.

Frederick Dorian, *The History of Music in Performance,* W. W. Norton.

Hans Rosenwald, "Changes in the Approach to Bach," *MTNA Proceedings,* volume XXXIV (1939).

Albert Schweitzer, *J. S. Bach,* Breitkopf und Härtel.

Charles S. Terry, *Bach's Orchestra,* Oxford University Press.

Donald F. Tovey, *Essays in Musical Analysis,* volume V, Oxford University Press.

Donald F. Tovey, *Musical Textures,* Oxford University Press.

W. G. Whittaker, *Fugitive Notes on Certain Cantatas and the Motets of J. S. Bach,* Oxford University Press.

W. G. Whittaker, "A Pilgrimage through the Church Cantatas of J. S. Bach," *Collected Essays,* Oxford University Press.

W. G. Whittaker, "Some Problems in the Performance

of Bach's Church Cantatas," *Proceedings of the Musical Association*, 54th session, 1927-1928.

G. Wallace Woodworth, "The Performance of Bach," Reprint, American Musicological Society, meeting of December 29-30, 1937.

Whether the director is returning to the actual size of the Bach chorus or not, he must keep in mind the sound ideal of the Baroque period in working out dynamic design. He must realize that the dynamic intensities should be those which might conceivably have been produced by a chorus of moderate, not gigantic, size, concertizing with, not accompanied by, an instrumental body of approximately equal power. The overpowering rush of tone which some choral conductors employ so vigorously is out of keeping with the Baroque style, as are the excessively whispering pianissimos which die away into virtual nothingness. Broad dynamic levels, conceived on an architectural basis, whose appeal is made through spacious proportions, rather than through spasmodic bursts of violent dynamic accentuations, constitute the fundamental element of the Baroque dynamic design.

The principles vital to a correct interpretation of Baroque choral literature may be summed up as follows:

a. Meter and tempo. The rhythmic pulse is to be delineated with firmness and decision. The pulsations are to be organized upon a generally metrical basis except in the case of recitative, where the organization of the pulsations follows the sequence of the prose accents. Some use is made of tempo rubato: early in the period, generally conforming with the principles of prose rhythm; during the High Baroque era, sparingly, chiefly in the nature of a broadening at the conclusion of the section.

b. Structural relationship between counterpoint and harmony. In case of definitely homophonic music: the chief melodic element is to be brought out, with the accompanying parts occupying a subordinate position. In contrapuntal music: the severally important voices are to be combined so that their independence is retained; the texture is to result from a combination of individually important voices whose relationship to each other takes on a vertical or harmonic implication.

c. Expressive quality of the score. The quality of the emotional expressiveness is to be determined by the coloristic possibilities of the word: early in the period, an underlining of the individually dramatic words; during the High Baroque, a projection of universal dramatic truths somewhat objectively viewed.

d. Dynamic scheme. Dynamic areas are to be depicted in wide strokes, large areas of a comparatively uniform color being employed, with the change in dynamics effected in general between sections rather than within the section. Relatively little use of the c r e s c e n d o as such is to be employed.

CHAPTER XIII

THE AGE OF CLASSICISM
1750-1825

With the passing of Bach and Handel from the scene at the middle of the eighteenth century, a new type of personality appears, not only in the field of musical activity but in all departments of life. The massive proportions of the Baroque edifice seem to have become oppressive to eighteenth-century man, and something is desired which is more casual and cheerful, less spacious and ceremonious. Intimacy rather than formality, lightness of touch rather than impressiveness of utterance — these appear to be the qualities most admired.

The word "rococo," borrowed from the field of the visual arts, in which it is used with particular reference to architecture and interior decoration, has been employed on occasion in other areas to refer to certain aspects of the eighteenth-century attitude. It usually implies delicacy of design, abundance of ornamentation, elegance of an intimate sort, and a general atmosphere of pleasant gaiety. Historically, the Rococo period is usually said to close with the French Revolution, the courts of Louis XV and XVI epitomizing the climax of the style.

Considered by some writers, notably Egon Friedell,[28] as a late phase of Baroque, Rococo constitutes a reaction against the overweening magnificence and solemnity of the former. The Rococo demonstrates a lightening of touch in all spheres. Taste and proportion are now favored above richness and size. Where the Baroque spirit had inclined toward grandiloquence of statement and seriousness of demeanor, the Rococo prefers animation in discourse and sprightliness of manner. The Rococo style brings a reduction in the emphasis upon a dramatic emotional expressiveness and turns toward the attainment of a purely formal beauty. The typical

---

28 *A Cultural History of the Modern Age*, transl. from the German by Charles Francis Atkinson, New York, Alfred A. Knopf, 1933, vol. II.

composer of the time attaches much importance to form, devoting great care to matters of arrangement and balance.

The Rococo spirit in music is exemplified in the *style galant*, originating in France during the first part of the eighteenth century with the clavecin school of François Couperin, 1668-1733. Georg Philipp Telemann, 1681-1767, and Domenico Scarlatti, 1685-1757, stand as exponents of the style in Germany and Italy respectively. The term *style galant* is usually applied to the secular style of the court and salon music of the day.

With Wilhelm Friedemann Bach, 1710-1784, and his brother Karl Philipp Emanuel, 1714-1788, there may be noted a transformation of the *style galant* into what is known as the *empfindsamer Stil* (sensitive style). The latter is characterized by a somewhat more personal expression of feeling than was possible in the rather conventionalized formulae of the *style galant*. It is evident that the *empfindsamer Stil* foreshadows the free emotional expression of nineteenth-century romanticism. With Franz Josef Haydn, 1732-1809, Classicism assumed a definite stylistic individuality by the fourth quarter of the century, combining traits of eighteenth-century Rococo, *style galant*, and *Empfindsamkeit*.

The Classic spirit finds its highest musical realization in the works of Haydn, of Wolfgang Amadeus Mozart, 1756-1791, and in the early writing of Ludwig van Beethoven, 1770-1827. Beethoven belongs to Classicism, although he also has been called a herald of Romanticism. This description is not unjust, since there is apparent, particularly during the latter part of his life, a turn of mind which is evident in nineteenth-century Romanticism. It has to do primarily with music as a means for the expression of individual feeling. In the *empfindsamer Stil* of the eighteenth century a new note had been sounded, that of the personal voice expressing the sentiment of individual man, as contrasted with the Baroque concept of man as a universal representative of the whole race. Although intimations of personal feeling are to be discerned in Haydn and Mozart, throughout the entire

Classic period such expression was subject to the demands of constructional principles. The structural form tended to act as a mold through which emotional content was to be shaped into a final esthetic product. With Beethoven the intrusion of the personal note becomes stronger.

In Haydn and Mozart content accommodates itself to the exigencies of structural laws, the same being more or less true in the early works of Beethoven. In Beethoven's later compositions form accommodates itself to the necessities of content as in most typically Romantic works. The contrast is between "organic" and "inorganic" form. By "inorganic" one intends to imply a pre-existent scheme through which the content flows without any considerable alteration of the structural detail. It is a form which has so crystallized that it is hardly affected by the interplay of the emotional current. Such is the concept toward which Classicism at least tends. Romanticism, on the other hand, inclines toward an organic principle, a formal structure developing according to the content. In other words, the form develops as the work proceeds, being bound by no rigid, predetermined rules.

a. Meter and tempo. The pulsation is rather more delicately marked in Classic music than in music of the Baroque period. As a rule it proceeds with a more buoyant step and with somewhat more elegance of movement. The sprightliness and the vivacity of the Rococo spirit are reflected in the crisp precision of Classic rhythmic patterns. The choral conductor will find it necessary to employ a lighter beat with late eighteenth-century music than with that of the preceding era, at the same time delineating the meter with decision and relative steadiness. The ritardando and the accelerando are of somewhat more frequent occurrence in the music of the Rococo period. Rubato is still moderate and in no wise approaches the decided tempo alterations of succeeding eras. The delineation of the pulsation should be elastic and flexible. There should be a quality of give-and-take in the succession of the beats, but no sense of departure from the regularity of the metrical course. Transition from one tempo to another should take on the character of a slight bending of the pulse; it implies a leaning to one side or the other rather than a change in the course of the beat.

b. Structural relationship between counterpoint and harmony. Once more counterpoint tends to fall into the discard, this time supplanted by purely melodic considerations. The *style galant* was particularly addicted to melody *per se.* So complete was the supremacy of melody that the bass line lost some of the independence of the thorough-bass period and at times became merely a prop for the principal upper voice. Other voices than the one entrusted with the melody and the supporting bass tended to receive scant attention with the result that, strictly speaking, contrapuntal interest often disappears from the typical eighteenth-century score. With the Classicism of Haydn and Mozart there is evident a revival of interest in contrapuntal writing, although it is quite clear that the counterpoint is usually developed from a generally harmonic basis.

The passion for ornament so characteristic of Rococo style evidenced itself in the abundance of decorative figures with which the melodic line was occasionally overladen. Used with discretion and applied with taste, the ornament was capable of imparting to music of the period a quality of fragility and delicate charm. Employed to excess it could smother the melody in meaningless flourishes.

The melodic curve of late eighteenth-century music tends toward greater brevity than that of the preceding epoch, the spacious contour of the Baroque arch being now replaced by a shorter span. Brief motives and fragmentary figures characterize the typically eighteenth-century melodic pattern. The composers of that century are notable for a new interest in graciousness of line. Considerable conjunct motion is employed, awkward intervals in the main being shunned. During the Classic period added interest is afforded through the increased employment of chromatic intervals.

Proper interpretation of eighteenth-century choral music presupposes on the part of the conductor susceptibility to the charm of ingratiating melody with the supporting voices treated in a generally unobtrusive fashion. For the music of Classicism the conductor will take particular note of the passages where contrapuntal texture appears. He will treat them so that the contrapuntal design is clearly drawn, but he will deal with the counterpoint in such a way that its vertical implications are smooth and yet varied in harmonic color.

c. Expressive quality of the score. Previous mention has been made of the importance of the *Affektenlehre* in evolving an interpretative scheme for music of the Baroque period. The doctrine had appeared as a subject for esthetic discussion in the seventeenth century. It was adopted as the artistic creed of the Rococo period, which saw a particular application of the principle in the *empfindsamer Stil*. Arising in the Baroque Era, coming to a point of high influence in the eighteenth century, it passed over with obvious ease into nineteenth-century Romanticism. The application of the theory, to be sure, was a highly conventionalized procedure, lacking the free individuality of Romanticism. Nevertheless, connections are to be noted between the basic concepts of these different historical periods.

It has been remarked that with the Rococo, particularly in its later phases, emotional utterance tends to take on a more personal tone. The universality of the Baroque emotional representation has been replaced by a more intimate avowal of feeling, especially in the *empfindsamer Stil* of the latter part of the eighteenth century. At the same time, the problem of form now comes to the fore. Less importance is attached to content and more to structural perfection. Manner and mode of utterance become problems of great moment. Emphasis is placed on correctness of style, elegance of speech, on the reproduction of the politely conversational tone rather than on the thundering dramatic proclamation. The absence of dramatic rhetoric is not to be mistaken for lack of feeling. Neither should the emphasis on sprightliness and gaiety obscure the skill of the craftsmanship. Gentility, poise, grace of gesture, these are essential aspects of Rococo art.

The Rococo spirit dislikes extravagant emotional representation, considering it tasteless. Whereas in the Baroque period dramatic antagonisms were expressed with passionate vehemence at times, the Rococo as a matter of habit tends to represent them with moderation and discretion. In the early Rococo, dramatic emotion is stated not passionately but formally. Remoteness and detachment in the observation of emotional conflict are characteristic attitudes, particularly as observable in the *style galant*. The formalistic approach to emotional representation is reflected in the more or less set vocabulary of the *Affektenlehre*. The quality of superficiality which some attribute to Rococo art is due not to emotional insensitivity but rather to the fact that the Rococo, instead of revealing itself directly, tends to speak through an established formula.

In choral works of the early eighteenth century — the period of the later Baroque — the conductor should note the emphatic expression of intense emotional interplay. He will observe as he proceeds through the seventeenth century a lessening in emotional intensity. As he approaches the Rococo period, he should employ a more detached and impersonal reading, one usually characterized by deftness of utterance. He will again note a turn in the characteristic emotional representation of the period of Classicism, wherein is to be felt a warmer, more personal expression, but one still characterized by a certain sense of decorum and reserve.

d. Dynamic scheme. The long crescendo and diminuendo become effective as dynamic devices in choral literature in the late eighteenth century. The long crescendo — known as the *Mannheim crescendo* by virtue of its extensive and expert use in the hands of the Mannheimers — is a mark of the Rococo style, appearing frequently in Mozart. However, the swelling and the diminishing of the tone are moderate in degree. The changes are likely to be gradual, with upper and lower limits less pronounced in intensity than those of later periods. The crescendo in particular does not reach the great dynamic heights of successive styles nor does it start from as low a dynamic level as is later customary.

By way of summary, the following points are of particular importance in approaching the choral music of the Classic period:

a. Meter and tempo. The rhythmic pulse is to be crisply and precisely felt, more or less regularly as in the Baroque period, but with less accentual weight. While the rhythmic organization is for the most part metrical, elasticity of movement is somewhat more frequent than in Baroque music.

b. Structural relationship between counterpoint and harmony. In music of the *style galant* and *Empfindsamkeit* prominence is to be given the melodic line, with supporting voices occupying a more or less subordinate position. As the Classic style comes to a climax during the closing years of the century, the performer must be more alert to contrapuntal relationships, as well as to the color afforded by harmonic scheme, melodic development and chromatic elements.

c. Expressive quality of the score. Emotional expression in the Classic period inclines toward a delicate, sensitive and rather humanly personal presentation of inner content, yet not giving itself up in the abandonment characteristic of nineteenth-century style.

d. Dynamic scheme. The terrace dynamics of the Baroque period give way to a system characterized by variation within the phrase. The long crescendo and diminuendo come into popular use, but are so treated that the degree of variation is still relatively modest.

CHAPTER XIV

THE ROMANTIC MOVEMENT
1800-1875

The term "Romanticism" will here be employed to designate the characteristic thought and art patterns of the nineteenth century, not, as is done on occasion, in a general sense to indicate the more impulsive and subjective phases of the creative spirit in various historical eras.

Romanticism as a style originated toward the end of the eighteenth century. Goethe's statement of the difference in attitude between his approach to art and that of Schiller has often been taken to constitute the point of departure for the new movement. Eckermann reports a conversation with Goethe on March 21, 1830, in which the poet expressed himself as follows:

> The idea of the distinction between classical and romantic poetry, which is now spread over the whole world, and occasions so many quarrels and divisions, came originally from Schiller and myself. I laid down the maxim of objective treatment in poetry, and would allow no other; but Schiller, who worked quite in the subjective way, deemed his own fashion the right one, and to defend himself against me, wrote the treatise upon 'Naive and Sentimental Poetry.' [1795-1796.] He proved to me that I myself, against my will, was romantic, and that my 'Iphigenia,' through the predominance of sentiment, was by no means so classical and so much in the antique spirit as some people supposed.
>
> The Schlegels took up this idea, and carried it further, so that it has now been diffused over the whole world; and every one talks about classicism and romanticism — of which nobody thought fifty years ago.[29]

---

[29] *Conversations of Goethe with Eckermann and Soret,* transl. from the German by John Oxenford, London, George Bell, 1883, rev. ed., p. 467.

Romanticism as a movement, however, did not originate with Goethe and Schiller. There were signs of the Romantic turmoil in various departments of life and art long before Goethe had discoursed upon the matter. Julien Tiersot cites the usage of the word "Romantic" by Jean-Jacques Rousseau, 1712-1778, and its application to the music of Étienne-Nicolas Méhul, 1763-1817, in the *Chronique de Paris* in 1792.[30]

The movement itself represents a multiplicity of ideas. Any simple statement of the Romantic creed is an utter impossibility. However, the choral conductor or student of choral literature must examine at least a few of its more salient factors.

Most apparent as an aspect of the Romantic movement is a revolt against convention and authority. The absolutism of the Baroque Era had become so complete that under its dominance all life assumed the character of a conventionalized pattern. Conformity, adherence to a prescribed code, submission to power from above, these were the hallmarks of eighteenth-century society. It was against such authoritarianism that Romanticism revolted. The formality and the restraint of the Rococo period had led to a rigidity in life and conduct which was reflected in the art of the times. Rococo represented deference to established custom; Romanticism represents a swing of the pendulum away from the shackling restrictions of the preceding era. It constitutes a rebellion against the veneration of tradition. Henceforward one need no longer conform to a code; one must no longer bow down to supreme authority. Rather, one is now to be free; one is to follow the dictates of one's own heart and conscience. One is no longer to accept as valid for conduct rules and regulations laid down by others; one now determines his own course of action according to his own mind and moral sense.

Emphasis on the freedom of personality was a concomi-

---

30 "Music and the Centenary of Romanticism," transl., Frederick H. Martens, *Musical Quarterly*, XV (1929), 269.

tant of the revolt against authoritarianism. One must be oneself; one is no longer a type, a representative of the whole human race. One is now an individual man, experiencing the joys and sorrows of the individual person and expressing them in individual fashion.

Search for novelty is another aspect of the Romantic spirit. Tired of the repetitive phrases and stereotyped expressions of Rococo convention, the romanticist looks for new forms, new modes of expression. He finds delight in new and strange effects, the exotic, the bizarre. The norm is no more to be cherished as the absolute standard. Departure from the mean may quite possibly produce a new and interesting character.

Romanticism was a movement with a strong literary bias, which permeated all fields of endeavor. Literature, music, painting, sculpture, architecture, all received the full impact of the movement. All the arts are found revolting against conventionality, in casting off rules and refusing to accept any rigid esthetic dicta. Free expression of the individual soul, depiction of personal emotion are the aims of the Romantic artist. This freedom releases a new personal lyricism which sings through all the art of the day.

In music the structural concept of the eighteenth century is set aside. In its best utilization of the formalistic principle, the late Rococo period had employed form as a means for the expression of feeling. Form served the composer as a channel of communication. In its weaker moments Rococo art had tended to value form above content. Romanticism sees a reversal of this principle in the triumph of content over form. In Romanticism the approach is made from the opposite direction to that of the Rococo period. What is it that the composer wishes to say? That is the first question. The form then is shaped by the nature of the content and is handled freely with no necessary regard for strict adherence to the principles of construction *per se*. Hereafter personal feeling is to be communicated, not through the foreordained expressional idiom of the *Affektenlehre*, but through the characteristically idiomatic phraseology of the composer.

The quest for novelty frequently led the Romantic composer to various types of experimentation. Color now exists in its own right; it is not, as usually heretofore, an agent of expression, but is cultivated as an end in itself. New and strange chords, surprising harmonic successions, piquant and unusual rhythms, all add to the total picture. Heightened dynamic devices are calculated to startle the listener. Sudden stops and starts, unanticipated fermatas, precipitate changes of pace increase the sensation of excitement and provide color through variety. Phrases are spun out to unforeseen length or foreshortened unexpectedly. Cadences are avoided or, with more characteristic significance than before, resolved deceptively. The typical romanticist demonstrates a fondness for the elaboration of the minute detail, the working out of a small motive. A kaleidoscopic pattern often results from this exploitation of the coloristic possibility of the small item.

Ascertaining the performance practice of Romantic music presents comparatively little difficulty. In the first place, for most persons the field of common knowledge lies mainly in the realm of Romantic music, since most early training has been largely in that literature. Familiarity through actual contact has made the average person more at home with this music than with that of any other era. Secondly, music notation had reached such a point of technological efficiency by the nineteenth century that it was possible for the composer to indicate quite clearly how he would like his music to sound. Thirdly, nineteenth-century composers for the most part devoted considerable care to the representation of their performance intentions. Dynamic signs are supplied in detail, phrasing is indicated, changes in tempo are marked with comparative precision, so that it is relatively easy for the interpreter to apprehend from the written score at least the approximate intention of the composer. Until the nineteenth century, composers frequently supervised the preparation of their works for performance. Hence, many directions for the performers were given personally and it was not thought necessary to write them in the score. Often, too, composers were writing only for their immediate present and had no thought of the possible use of their works by posterity. Naturally they would supply only marks necessary for the performance of the moment, which would serve as reminders to themselves. It was relatively easy to remedy in the course of the rehearsal many deficiencies which the composer of the present day cannot observe in person and which he must anticipate.

The choral conductor is not likely to have great difficulty in apprehending the nineteenth century. The main problem is that, being most familiar with this style, he is apt to carry its methods over into the music of other eras. To superimpose nineteenth-century Romantic style upon the works of other periods is an anachronism which every conductor should strive to avoid.

For purposes of choral interpretation, the principles basic to the Romantic style are here presented as for the previous epochs.

a. Meter and tempo. Rhythmic organization as in the preceding era proceeds in the direction of metrical patterning. Much use, however, is made of the various devices of syncopation. One of the most prominent of these is an effect which is actually that of multiple meter although not always so indicated by a change of time signature. The Baroque rhythmic conception had been monometrical in character; that is, it had tended to employ one basic meter for a work or for a section. The second movement of the Brahms *Requiem* contains an interesting example of a change of meter without accompanying change of signature. The effect is heightened by a cross-rhythm set up between the combined soprano, alto, and tenor parts against the bass part. In the fourth movement of the same work there is again a change of meter without specific notational indication. Here the regular metrical pattern in the accompaniment in combination with the cross-rhythms of the vocal parts provides rhythmic interest.[31] Composers of the Modern period would probably employ a new time signature for many passages which in the Romantic period continue, as far as the notation is concerned, in a previously established meter while creating the auditory impression of a new metrical pattern.

Rhythmic alteration not only may imply establishing a new basic meter, but also may produce a dislocation of the accent in a passage of comparatively brief duration. Syncopation in all its forms is favored by the Romantic composers. Cross-rhythms are found in abundance. These devices add to the effect of novelty so eagerly sought. Preoccupation with rhythmic patterns is characteristic of the romanticist, designs of bewildering intricacy and variety of effect often being employed. Rhythmic surprise is a basic ingredient of the style.

The constant pace of the Baroque and Classic styles gives way to a quickly changing tempo in the Romantic Era. Modifications of speed are often brought about by the operation of a new word-idea upon the writer's imaginative faculties. As the mood changes, so does the tempo. Baroque music in particular avoided such sudden rhythmic changes, usually allowing only relatively slight differences in degree of motion. The romanticist indulges in extremes. He often varies from barely perceptible movement to breathless haste. He may leap from a slow tempo to a rapid one with great alacrity or from a fast tempo to a slower one, so that many times he seems to have come to a precipitate halt without preparation. Rapid movement frequently takes on the character of a headlong rush, the rhythms of the faster movements becoming at times almost frenetic. Slow tempi, on the other hand, tend toward extreme slowness, the rate occasionally so deliberate that motion is detected only as a faint stirring of the rhythmic pulse.

Tempo rubato comes into its own in the Romantic Era.

---

31 New York, G. Schirmer, p. 26, meas. 8-10; p. 54, meas. 6-12.

The rubato, however, demands a treatment which relates it to the over-all view of the work. It must not be allowed to become the controlling element in performance. Rubato should never be so excessive and so free as to distort the rhythmic pattern. It must be related to the harmonic progressions, to the development of the melodic line, to the evolution of the thought content, always subject to the limitations of the structural integrity of the work.

The accelerando and the ritardando are found more frequently than heretofore. Also, the degree of change of pace is more decided, the difference between the slower and the more rapid gradations of the ritardando and the accelerando being greater.

Tempo variation in Romantic music, as in the music of all periods, requires discrimination. It should not be applied unless indicated. When the score calls for a ritardando or an accelerando, the conductor will naturally comply. However, the sensation should usually be that of a hastening or a slackening of the pulse, not, ordinarily, a wrenching of the fundamental pulsation. If a sudden change in tempo is intended by the Romantic composer, he will so indicate, but the indications should not be taken as license for extreme alteration of pace, as they too often are by the uninformed conductor.

The pulsation should be delineated firmly but with resilience and pliability. The sturdy, punctuated metrical beat of the Baroque Era has gone. In its place is a plastic sense of elasticity in the beat, a development of the tendency which had appeared during the Rococo period. At the same time, flexibility of beat should not be misinterpreted as formlessness in metrical design. The continuity of the current must be sustained, so that every pulse gives the sense of having progressed from the preceding one and advancing to the one that follows. The give-and-take, the slight emphasis here and there, the falling away at one point and another, are to be determined by the relative importance of the word-ideas, by the significance of individual tones in the melodic contours, by the place of the chord in the harmonic scheme. The pulse may change in speed, it may quicken, it may slacken, rush with headlong excitement, or walk with grave deliberation, but it must never come to a dead halt; it must not be allowed to die. Even in the fermata there should be a sense of rhythmic urgency, of reaching a point of gravity in the rhythmic progression, or of expectancy of the following movement. The rests, also, must have rhythmic vitality; they must not become mere blank spaces in the sound pattern, but must possess a quality of pulsation bearing a rhythmic relation to the sounds preceding and following. The alterations of tempo, the abundant ritardandos and accelerandos, the held chords, all have a tendency to obliterate the sense of rhythmic design unless treated with care. The conductor must so handle the fluctuating rhythmic movement that the composition possesses unity, that there is a sense of related rhythmic progression throughout the entire work, that the piece is not allowed to fall apart into a number of disjointed rhythmic scraps.

   b. Structural relationship between counterpoint and harmony. In the nineteenth century, harmony comes to the fore as the element of prime importance. The typically Romantic composer adopts a concept of texture dependent upon a harmonic basis. He normally thinks of the work in terms of harmony in rhythmic movement, a progression of sound combinations through time. This preoccupation is reflected in the melody, which often appears to have been conceived as a product of the harmony. The interest in an ingratiating contour reawakened during the days of the *style galant* and continuing in the Romantic period concerns itself with the individual aspect of the line at a given moment, in possible relation to a harmonic setting. Consequently, Romantic melody usually lacks the forthrightness of contrapuntal voice-leading which results from the driving forward of a horizontal line. The broad arches of essentially contrapuntal melody have been replaced by sinuousness of line and fluidity of curve within the microscopic melodic member.

The harmonic progression receives detailed and extensive treatment. New and unusual relationships, sudden harmonic changes, untried combinations are explored and extended. The physical and acoustical qualities of the chord are investigated; experiments are made with new qualities of sound within the chord. Dissonance is an important component, freely introduced and freely handled. Non-harmonic tones are plentiful, often resolved in unorthodox manner; appoggiaturas, suspensions, passing tones are common items of the nineteenth-century vocabulary. Chromaticism as applied both to chordal structure and to melodic outline adds to the richness of the palette. As contrasted with the practice of the eighteenth century, the harmonic system seems to be in a state of ferment, of perpetual flux.

The romanticist has a greater concern for sonority than for counterpoint. The contrapuntal aspect of the design tends to be submerged in harmonic considerations, linear quality often obscured by the harmonic material with which it is surrounded. The result is that the counterpoint, like the individual melody, seems to be an outgrowth of the harmonic structure rather than, as much earlier, operating as germ of the harmonic system. Even in passages of a predominantly contrapuntal character, one is frequently aware of the vertical implications. The treatment of counterpoint is such that the listener is inclined to hear it as a combination of lines coming together in harmonic patterns, not a series of horizontal melodies moving coincidentally together, as was the case with earlier polyphony. There is obvious in the Romantic scores a predilection for complexity of texture, for massiveness of structure. Largeness of tone is an apparent goal of the age, a largeness which is not always a matter of volume but often the result of the employment of *divisi* technique (division of voices and instrumental choirs into many parts).

The Baroque period had seen the vertical aspect of the contrapuntal texture assert itself. This development continued more markedly in the Romantic period. It has been said that at the time of Bach there was a state of equilibrium between counterpoint and harmony. The balance is now destroyed; the Romantic concept favors a state in which the harmonic element is the stronger.

Whereas the Baroque contrapuntist is concerned with the opposition of lines, the romanticist is concerned with the opposition of masses. Where the Baroque composer weaves a combination of lines into a total fabric, the romanticist places blocks of tone in opposition to each other and engraves the lines upon them. The texture of the best Baroque counterpoint is clear and transparent with the lines cleanly etched one against the other. The texture of Romantic counterpoint, on the other hand, is inclined to be full and thick. Purely contrapuntal sections as such are comparatively infrequent in occurrence, and usually brief when they do appear.

The liking of the romanticist for sudden changes, for the juxtaposition of a multiplicity of small items within the larger whole, is to be seen in the new aspect of the texture. The Baroque — and to a certain degree the Classic — concept involved the relation of relatively large areas, each comparatively uniform within itself. Contrast was obtained by the juxtaposition of areas of differing texture and style. In Romantic music the large area usually is subdivided into a number of smaller contrasting units. Classicism and Baroque see the work in relation to its existence as a large whole; Romanticism is inclined to view it as an association of diverse constituent elements. Donald Tovey speaks of the fact that certain works of Bach, for instance, "... produce much of their cumulative effect by their refusal to change their texture."[32] With the romanticist, on the other hand, a large part of the total effect is created by the more or less rapid alternation of textures within a comparatively short time. In the Romantic Era quicker alternations of homophonic and contrapuntal material appear than formerly. The counterpoint

---

[32] *Musical Textures* (A Musician Talks, vol. II), London, Oxford University Press, 1941, p. 44.

breaks off into a purely harmonic passage or else dissolves into homophonic-contrapuntal imitation. Imitation is generally fragmentary in nature, being more harmonic-melodic than purely contrapuntal in concept.

c. Expressive quality of the score. A new quality of personal expressiveness appears in the Romantic scores. Again, as always, it is linked to the word-idea. Word-idea and emotional expression were connected during the Renaissance, but then the expression inclined toward a pictorial-descriptive representation of a more or less stylized situation or personage. Emotional expressiveness was a vital constituent of the Baroque style, but the expression was that of the individual as representative of the universal type, caught in the conflict of forces which to a large degree were outside himself. The struggle was one operating upon him as member of the race, not the strife of an individual human soul. In Romanticism the personally human note is strongly sounded. No more is it a pictorial representation of a stylized emotional situation, nor humanity caught in the maelstrom of the fates. Now it is personal man waging a solitary contest against whatever powers surround him and threaten his independence of expression and action.

Man is found in the midst of emotional turmoil, a turmoil engendered by the forces of nature, by the clash of human personalities, expressed in love, fear, hatred, and all the microcosmic catalogue of human passions — a turmoil which, engendered by no matter what means, verges on the turbulent and intense. The degree of emotionalism is scarcely ever moderate in the typically Romantic artist; it tends toward the extreme.

Man in the midst of nature is a favorite subject of the romanticists — man alone on a mountain top, in the depths of the forest, by a roaring cataract, by the abnormally still waters of an abnormally quiet lake — man alone in the midst of nature with thunders cracking over his head, lightning flashing around his forehead, rain beating upon his brow — man alone, dreaming in the heat of a sun which burns fierce-

ly upon him — man to whom the birds sing messages of un-
utterable joy and sadness — man at twilight with the melancholy stillness of evening closing around him — man in the
moonlight drunk with the strange perfume of thousands of
exotic blossoms — man in the throes of violent passion, to
whom love is ecstasy and the denial of love is death — man
whose joy is frenetic, whose sorrow is deepest tragedy —
man to whom nothing seems to happen in moderation, to whom
everything appears to occur upon a high level of excitement.
The Romantic movement is related to the literary movement
of *Sturm und Drang* (Storm and Stress), whose designation
constitutes a sufficiently clear indication of its character.

To intensify the emotional implications of his texts,
the Romantic composer draws on every resource. Chromatics
adorn the melodic line, emphasizing the dramatic content
with their colors. Soaring melodic curves bound off into
space, amazing parabolas of surprising amplitude, contrasted
with terse melodic motives pungent in their emotional directness. Strange intervallic relationships serve as agents of
dramatic expression. Appoggiaturas, suspensions, all manner
of foreign tones build up the emotional tension. Rhythms
produce excitement through the vigor of their accents, through
the magnetic power of cross-rhythms, the electrifying quality
of terrific speed, contrasted with a slowness which is barely
perceptible as motion. Rich, colorful harmonic patterns build
up the emotional and dramatic effect. Tremendous climaxes,
thunderous outbursts of tone are followed by the hush of
barely audible pianississimos. Every resource of the musical
vocabulary is made an agency of mood representation.

The difference between the Baroque and Romantic techniques of emotional expression is to be observed in the manner in which the word-idea acts as stimulus to the creative
musicians of the two eras. In both periods the motivating
factor in establishing the quality of the expression is the
word with reference to its *(a)* pictorial or descriptive powers,
(b) dramatic or emotional connotations, or *(c)* psychological
or spiritual implications. A salient pictorial word may act

as mainspring to the creative process, one basic idea serving as the germinating force of a movement or section. No matter how the word functions — as pictorial or descriptive factor, as dramatic or emotional stimulus, as associative psychological or spiritual impulse — its sphere of influence is extended over a comparatively large area in typically Baroque style.

The romanticist, on the other hand, shows a high degree of susceptibility to fluctuating emotional values. Stylistic changes occur rapidly as a result of the appearance of new textual ideas. A movement, having embarked upon a definite and characteristic stylistic path, may be halted or deflected into an entirely different direction by the sudden appearance in the text of a new idea. Rather than employing one basic thought as germane to the entire movement or section, the Romantic composer is quite likely to seize upon a number of ideas, which may follow each other in at times bewildering succession, changing the entire structure abruptly.

In the Baroque period the range of moods is reasonably simple and uncomplicated; with the romanticist the scope of the emotional range is much wider. He not only often experiences a variety of moods in a brief period of time, he also customarily experiences each changing mood with a remarkable degree of intensity. The Romantic expression of joy becomes at times a frenzy of exultation, in contrast to its delineation in the music of Bach, for instance, where it may be strong and affirmative but never unleashed. Similarly with the darker moods. Tragedy is expressed by Bach with quiet resignation, in uncomplaining acceptance and patient submission. With the romanticist, tragedy often calls forth the expression of a violent emotional upheaval, the experience of an intensely personal and bitter grief.

d. Dynamic scheme. The nineteenth century sees a great expansion of the dynamic range. In place of the terrace dynamics of the Baroque, there has developed a system of gradation dynamics in which the transition from one level to another is made, not by an immediate step to a new level up or down as formerly, but through a gradual progression from one degree to another. The long crescendo – which had been employed with great skill by the Mannheim group in the eighteenth century – is extended and becomes common practice in the nineteenth century.

The extremes of the dynamic register are exploited, much use being made of fortissimo and pianissimo, in contrast to the customary practice of the preceding era which in the main had confined itself to a mere alternation of forte and piano with an occasional fortissimo for increased emphasis or an occasional pianissimo for heightened effect. Fortississimo *(fff)* and pianississimo *(ppp)* are not uncommon in the music of the Romantic Era. The Ricordi edition of the *Manzoni Requiem* by Verdi even calls for the extremes of *ppppp* and *pppppp*.[33]

The tension provided by dynamic extremes is increased by accents of various types, strong dynamic stress being an attribute of Romantic treatment. The sforzando appears with great frequency in the Romantic score. It is often of such percussive effect that writing for voices takes on the quality of an instrumental style.

The sound ideal of the Romantic Era is that of a large vocal force combined with a large orchestra to produce a tone of massive quality and rich texture. The old polyphonic *a cappella* concept has given way to a choral-orchestral practice for the most part as the representative mode of choral expression. The ideal is not unaccompanied vocal color, nor choral-instrumental duplication, but vocal-instrumental timbres combined, with the total fabric emerging from the opposition of color masses. As a general rule, the choral and orchestral forces are maintained as separate entities. The choral lines are customarily superimposed on the background provided by the instrumental parts. The instrumental score usually fills a subordinate role as accompaniment to the choral forces, no longer concertizing with the vocal lines in the equality of the Baroque style, but occupied

---

33 Milan, London, pp. 118, 179, 211.

with its own particularly idiomatic expression. Large choruses and large orchestras become the fashion. Consequently
there is a certain increased generosity in the outpouring of
tone in the Romantic age. The reticence of earlier days is
dispelled in a free release of the tonal volume.

The Romantic emphasis on sonority entails a mounting
concern with the physical quality of the tone. This concentration on physical quality produces a largeness of timbre
which brings the higher dynamic levels into frequent play.
The thickness of texture, the utilization of nuance, the cap-
italizing on the juxtaposition of dynamic contrast, together
with the addition of resources make possible a sonority of
great richness and brilliance.

The principles involved in the proper interpretation of
the choral music of the Romantic Era may be summarized as
follows:

a. Meter and tempo. The metrical patterning of the rhythmic pulsation is to be maintained. However, there should
be a sense of plasticity and flexibility in the delineation
of the beat. A more abundant use of tempo rubato is employed
than in the literature of preceding eras. Alternations of
speed are to be expected. The quality of rhythmic continuity is to be preserved throughout the course of the work,
all alterations of tempo being so accomplished that the
pulse retains its quality of vitality. The hastening and slackening of pace are to be executed as indicated, but never
with the loss of rhythmic unity and of continuity of progression. The authority of the score is to be respected in matters
of tempo, particularly with regard to alterations of speed
and to the application of the tempo rubato. The conductor
customarily does not need to add to the markings supplied
by the composer. He only needs to consider carefully the
indications supplied and then to apply them in performance
in the way that seems most in keeping with the spirit and
style of the work.

*b. Structural relationship between counterpoint and har-
mony.* The conductor will be alert to the harmonic implica-

tions of the score. He will emphasize the harmonic character of the structure, giving as a matter of custom a reading recognizing the predominantly harmonic concept of the period. He will be particularly observant of chromatic chords and those of an unusual construction. Contrapuntal passages will be performed with due regard for imitative material. In fugal passages the statement of the subject should be slightly emphasized as is the case with the music of any period in which the imitative technique is employed. The principal idea should not be accented so heavily as to distort the musical architecture but sufficiently to provide the corner-stone of the section involved. Non-harmonic tones such as appoggiaturas, suspensions, and passing tones, are to be treated so that their relationship to the harmonic structure is preserved and their special potentialities realized.

c. Expressive quality of the score. Although the portrayal of the human and personal reaction reaches a high point in the literature of the Romantic period, the interpreter must not allow his depiction of the emotional element to become excessively subjective and over-personal. While intensity of feeling should characterize the performance of this music, it must never be allowed to get out of bounds, but must always maintain a sense of balance and of equilibrium. This is the one element which the average choral director apparently finds most difficult to control. Human feeling must be portrayed with sympathy and warmth; it must be represented with keen insight into the individual and personal problem. Yet the portrayal of this feeling should never be allowed to become an exhibitionistic parading of private emotion for public effect. It should always be characterized by decorum and dignity.

Furthermore, it should not become so peculiarly personal that it loses contact with humanity as a whole. One should keep in mind that the highest Romantic concept is the identification of personal experience with that of humanity at large. When the expression of experience loses this quality of universality, it ceases to be a fit subject for art.

d. Dynamic scheme. The conductor is permitted a freedom in the releasing of dynamic energy heretofore unattained. Higher and lower levels of tone are employed than ever before in the history of choral literature. Crescendos and diminuendos are allowedly extensive. Sudden climaxes are a feature of the style. Dynamic accents are vigorous and emphatic. The contrast obtained by placing in close proximity sections of widely differing dynamic values is a part of the Romantic vocabulary. Nevertheless, the conductor is to be warned that freedom is not to be confused with license, that release is not to be confounded with capriciousness, that only in service to a reasonable law is true freedom to be found.

CHAPTER XV

THE MODERN PERIOD
1875 TO THE PRESENT

Whether the twentieth century represents a new stage in the historical development of cultures or whether it is one aspect of a total larger movement of which the nineteenth century may also be a part, it is not possible to discern at this too close point of observation. The perspective of history is needed in order to conclude whether Modernism is a new and separate tendency, herald of a new age to follow, or whether the trends of the twentieth century constitute a possibly late phase of previous developments.

As time goes on, historians have a tendency to look at cultural movements in ever broadening chronological periods. The Renaissance was at one time considered a sudden revival of interest in learning taking place somewhat inexplicably at about 1500 and continuing its glorious reign for a space of some one hundred years. The cinquecento was thought an adequate period of time to embrace the expressions of the Renaissance spirit. Later writers have inclined to push the date of beginning further and further back. Friedell is "... forced to the conclusion that the 'conception' of the new age occurred in Italy, as elsewhere, about the middle of the fourteenth century."[34] Leichtentritt sees even earlier intimations when he says, "The youthful romantic spirit of the twelfth century marks the dawn of the Italian Renaissance. It is the immediate precursor of this great movement."[35] Cecil Gray advances the idea that the Baroque movement may be a phase of the Renaissance, that Romanticism may be merely a trend in the current set up during the the eighteenth century, that the present period may constitute another angle of Romanticism.[36] It well may be that

34 *A Cultural History,* I, 154.

35 *Music, History, and Ideas,* p. 62.

36 *A Survey of Contemporary Music,* London, Oxford University Press, 1924, pp. 255-256.

166

succeeding generations, surveying their past from a longer perspective, will say that the whole course of history and of art since the close of the Middle Ages constitutes one large cultural sweep which is the period of the Renaissance. Within that frame of reference the Baroque period and the Age of Enlightenment, Romanticism, Realism, Modernism, and all such terms would constitute merely tags marking not separate divisions of the stream of history but rather tributary factors, the total confluence of which comprises one historical development.

Whether Romanticism is considered as separate from the Renaissance or a further development of its fundamental attitudes, whether the twentieth century is an aspect of late Romanticism or not, the consideration of the characteristics peculiar to each of these periods is of value in coming to an understanding of the art of each and of a method proper to its interpretation.

Even though Modernism may be a phase of the Romantic trend, nevertheless the current of life during the last quarter of the nineteenth century underwent a change that is reflected in the arts of the time. This change may be taken as indicative of a new mode of expression in music. It marks the formulation of a new style designated as "Impressionism," which exhibits certain reactions against the then prevailing Romanticism. Impressionism as a herald of twentieth-century Modernism is a point upon which musical scholars have not agreed. The style is taken by some writers to mark the beginning of the modern epoch of music history, while by others it is considered a type of late Romanticism. Similar disagreement appears over musical "Nationalism," which is held by some to be evidence in the latter part of the nineteenth century of a new and "modern" spirit, while others regard it as properly belonging to the Romantic period.

For the purposes of the present-day choral conductor, Impressionism may be taken to mark the beginning of a style, which in its revolt against certain aspects of Romanticism may be said to belong to the Modern period. As Romanticism was an artistic movement in which music and literature were closely joined, so Impressionism bears an intimate relationship to contemporary trends in painting. As a musical style, Impressionism arises in the last quarter of the nineteenth century with Claude Debussy, 1862-1918. Maurice Ravel, 1875-1937, represents a continuance of the style.

Impressionism first of all constitutes a reaction against the highly colored and intense emotionalism of late nineteenth-century Romanticism. To the deeply personal contortions of the uninhibited romanticist, the impressionist opposes reserve in expression, a restraint and delicacy of emotional statement. Reticence rather than release characterizes the style. To the warm and richly colored harmonic palette of the Romantic style, Impressionism opposes the cooler pastel tones, translucent and clear in character. To the strong impulses of Romantic rhythmic movement, Impressionism opposes a floating, often vague, indefiniteness of motion. In general, Impressionism is an art of delicacy, reserve, shyness, and restraint. No violent highlightings, no more the dramatic juxtaposition of light and dark or the sudden contrast of day and night; rather, the half-lights of dawn and twilight. In place of the emotional oratory of late Romanticism, the impressionist supplies the slight suggestion of only dimly realized emotional thrusts and counterthrusts. Understatement rather than dramatic emphasis is customary.

It is manifestly impossible to reduce all the various tendencies of the twentieth century to one or even a few stylistic trends. However, it is possible to examine with profit, even if briefly, some of the tendencies that have been most potent in their effect upon the development of characteristic styles in the Modern Era. A survey of the most assertive tendencies reveals three more or less clearly perceptible points of change in the conception of musical structure from about 1875 to the present. Impressionism constitutes the first. A second change is apparent about 1910-1912 with the movement called "Expressionism." Around 1925 a third movement known as "Neo-classicism" assumes prominence as a mode of expression.

Expressionism appears about 1910 with Arnold Schoenberg, 1874-1951, and his followers, Alban Berg, 1885-1935, Anton von Webern, b. 1883, Egon Wellesz, b. 1885, and Ernst Křenek, b. 1900. This movement, like Impressionism, is observable in music and literature, reflecting influences which were particularly strong in the field of painting. It constitutes, first, a reaction against the vague indefiniteness of Impressionism. The blurring of outline and smudging of detail, the understatement characterizing Impressionism are replaced by sharper delineations of line, a firmer grasp of the rhythmic movement, and a bolder manner of utterance.

A difference is to be noted in the manner in which the two types of stylistic expression originate. The Impressionistic work of art may be said to result from the operation upon the artist's creative faculties of an impulse which comes to him from without. The "impression" which that outer object makes upon his inner consciousness is represented in terms of a symbol — visual, musical, or literary — which is calculated to arouse within the spectator, the auditor, or the reader the state of mind and feeling which the stimulus first aroused within the creator. On the other hand, the Expressionistic work of art may be said to proceed from the operation on the creative faculties of the artist of an inner, subjective emotion or idea of his own. Hence the *ex*pression that comes out of the creator toward the onlooker or the listener in a pattern formulated by the inner feeling of the artist. Reference may be made to Adolfo Salazar's discussion of Impressionism and Expressionism in his book *Music in Our Time.*[37]

By the manipulation of the technical tools of the musician's trade — melodic configuration, harmonic combinations, rhythmic motives — the Expressionistic composer seeks an *ex*pression of an inner state or reaction. Colors, forms, rhythmic groupings, harmonies, lines — all the devices and formulae of his art — are employed to evolve a design that makes no attempt at realistic representation, but seeks to

---

37 Transl. Isabel Pope, New York, W. W. Norton, 1946.

express the working of the artist's inner consciousness in terms of an external art. Hence the use by the Expressionistic artist of what to the uninitiated may seem an abstract pattern. In Impressionism the original impulse comes from without inward; in Expressionism it proceeds outward from within.

The third phase of modern music, that of Neo-classicism, may be considered as opening in 1923 with Igor Stravinsky's *Octuor for Wind Instruments*. This phase represents a return of the structural ideal as the motivating force in composition. Emphasis is placed on solving the problem of form. Thus the pendulum swings again to a consideration of form over content, to a conception in which the composer looks toward the manipulation of materials without necessarily giving attention to expressive content as such. Form receives the primary emphasis; expression of feeling is a resultant, secondary consideration. Stravinsky, b. 1882, in works of his later period, and Paul Hindemith, b. 1895, represent the leadership of the style.

Various tendencies appear from time to time in the Modern period as characteristic trends. Most of them do not coalesce into such definiteness that they can be said to constitute clearly defined movement. "Realism" is one such tendency, appearing in the latter part of the nineteenth century with the music of Richard Strauss, 1864-1949, and continuing to appear intermittently throughout the period. Realistic suggestion has been employed often in the course of music history. In fact, there are few periods in which it does not appear in some guise. Waterfalls, birdcalls, portraits of Lady This and Lady That, battles, duels, hunting scenes, and what not have through the ages been popular subjects for musical treatment.

However, the difference between the Realism of earlier days and that of the twentieth century lies primarily in the importance it assumes in the musical scheme. Until the late nineteenth century Realism was largely limited to suggestion. Realistic devices employed earlier were appurtenances of the musical expression, utilized to heighten the dramatic effect, to make the emotional signification more telling. With Strauss and subsequent exponents of the style the aim of rendering emotional expression more meaningful is often supplanted by what appears to be an aim at purely graphic description.

Contemporary Realism often may be described as representational in character, occupied with the faithful depiction in music of external situations, the description of external objects. No mention need be made of the countless examples of Realism which have poured from the pens of composers during the past half-century: rushing water, galloping horsemen, cataracts, torrents, locomotives, airplane propellers, factory noises, all described in music with unmistakable accuracy.

"Verismo" is the Italian version of Realism. It appears in opera in 1890 with Mascagni's *Cavalleria Rusticana*. The realism here is the realism of natural life. The subjects of Veristic opera are no longer the gods and half-gods, the superhumanly noble personages, the exalted luminaries of eighteenth- and nineteenth-century opera, but ordinary persons depicted in the common routine of life. The subject is usually placed in a highly dramatic situation and the treatment is customarily melodramatic in tone. Verismo in music is not unrelated to the literary movement known as "Naturalism." *Carmen* is often cited as an example of Verismo; *Pagliacci* is also Veristic in treatment.

"Futurism" is a type of realism particularly concerned with industrial subjects. It has a parallel in painting, which may be described briefly as primarily concerned with the representation of the subject in motion rather than in static repose. Futurism in music aims at conveying to the auditor the sense of the movement of an object. Dynamos, wheels in motion, trains in transit are favorite subjects for the Futuristic artist.

"Mechanism." The mechanistic character of twentieth-century civilization has made a strong impact upon the various arts. Its influence is most clearly apparent in matters of design and structure. New constructions in form and arrangement, the development of harmonic systems, the evolution of melodic contours often reflect a mechanistic spirit of experimentation.

What are the implications of these various trends for the interpreter of choral literature? First of all, the conductor must consider whether a work is actually modern or not. Mere chronology does not serve as proof. A piece written well after 1900 may be thoroughly Romantic in spirit. In fact much choral literature which appears on programs as modern is not at all contemporaneous in spirit, being more closely affiliated to previously prevailing forms and styles than to those particularly characteristic of the present day. If the work is to be considered truly modern it must use the techniques and vocabulary of twentieth-century Modernism. If, although written in the past few years, it still clings to a belated Romanticism, then the principles of twentieth-century interpretative style do not properly belong to it and it should be interpreted according to the nineteenth-century tradition. If, however, it is essentially contemporary in tone and spirit, then it must be given a treatment setting it apart as a work belonging to a style different from those of preceding eras.

a. Meter and tempo. With Impressionism there is a relaxation of the rhythmic energy which in general characterizes the Romantic style. In place of the firmly beating rhythmic pulse there is now a lessening of tension in the movement. Romantic vigor gives way to a faintly throbbing beat.

The organization of the pulsations into metrical patterns becomes much less regular in character. The metrical patterning is often less bold, less obvious, and less confined by concern for uniformity. Multiple meter, already evident in Romantic works though often not indicated in the score, becomes a prominent feature of this style. Strong dynamic or stress accent occurs with comparative infrequency in Impressionistic music.

The sudden alterations of tempo which were so important in Romantic rhythmic treatment do not usually appear in Impressionism. Transitions from one tempo to another are made more infrequently than in Romanticism and are accomplished with less suddenness. In general, extremely rapid tempos are avoided, the rate inclining toward the moderate and the slow. When rapidity is demanded, it is accomplished with a sense of lightness and deftness as contrasted with the headlong rush of the typically Romantic fast tempos.

The conductor will employ a less vigorous beat with Impressionistic music than is customarily used with Romantic. He will feel under no compulsion to set up strictly ordered metrical successions. Comparatively little use will ordinarily be made of accent as such. Accent will usually be replaced by a buoyancy and fluidity of rhythm which will keep the work in motion but will be so flexible that there is no sense of binding or restricting the pulsation by regularity of pattern.

One of the most obvious aspects of the reaction of Expressionism against what was felt to be the formlessness of Impressionism is a new sense of rhythmic directness, a greater incisiveness in the delineation of the rhythmic pulsations. Multiple meter is frequently encountered with what appears to be a total lack of concern with regularity of metrical pattern and of sequential metrical successions. Much attention is given to speech values, with the result that the rhythmic patterns of the music correspond in general to the prose rhythms of the text.

As music proceeds through the Modern Era, increased interest is evidenced in pure rhythm as such. Rhythm is elaborated and developed in much the same way that counterpoint was explored in the late Renaissance. Rhythmic complexities of all kinds abound in the various types of modern writing. Beats are freely combined: two, three, four, five, seven, even one to the bar succeeding each other, obeying no foreordained law of regular succession. This concern with a musical element as a problem to be investigated seems to take first place at times with the Neo-classic composer, supplanting what had in other eras been a primary preoccupation with music as an agent of expression.

After brief remission in Impressionism, rhythmic tension, vitality, and energy increase during the Modern period. One of the most apparent characteristics of modern music is its rhythmic drive, its sense of rhythmic urgency. Inexorable, inescapable rhythms pound through the twentieth century, often fierce and savage in their insistency. Rhythmic pulsations are set up and reiterated furiously, combined in ever-changing and shifting arrangements, which by the mere fact of their variation make the driving force more intense. Harmonic effects are crushed in upon the listener constantly by the sheer impact of the rhythmic force.

The rhythmic germ is often a terse, epigrammatic motive. Its brevity, combined with the insistence of reiteration, makes it all the more dynamic. Ceaseless repetition of the short, incisive motive united with a fierceness of declamation constitutes the vitalizing force of a large number of contemporary works. Modern music nearly always possesses the quality of "going somewhere"; even if occasionally without knowing exactly where, it is at least on the way. Dynamism, movement, speed, activity are characteristics of twentieth-century life and of much twentieth-century music. Social historians are fond of making comparisons between the restlessness, the tensions, the conflicts of the vortex of the age and the dynamic love of physical motion which is evident in much present-day art. The interpreter of twentieth-century literature must, first of all, take cognizance of its rhythmic vitality and adroitness.

  b. *Structural relationship between counterpoint and harmony*. The harmonic preoccupation of the romanticist is intensified in the impressionist. Counterpoint as such virtually disappears as an element of the musical fabric. The chord becomes an object of primary consideration and may now exist for itself alone. Attention is often shifted from the previously prevailing consideration of the chord in relation to other chords to a consideration of the chord as a separate entity. The single chord is dwelt upon and exploited for all the possibilities of expansion which may exist within it. The impressionist's interest in harmony for its own sake is comparable to the preoccupation of the later contemporary composer with rhythm for its own sake.

All sorts of new chords appear, and all manner of new treatments of chords in relation to each other. Seventh chords of various types and chords of the ninth are common in Impressionistic composition, and chords of the eleventh and thirteenth are by no means infrequent. Parallel motion of intervals and chords is a mark of the Impressionistic style. A new organum of parallel octaves and fifths appears. Chords in parallel motion — the so-called gliding or sliding chords — impart a new harmonic tang.

The conductor of Impressionistic choral literature must be alive to the harmonic values of the work with which he is dealing. He must be particularly alert for the accurate intonation of Impressionistic music, which presents a problem for the average singer. The intervals upon first acquaintance often seem curious; the intervallic relationships and successions are unexpected; the harmonic combinations produce an effect not attained in the era preceding Impressionism. The manner in which chords are strung together, gliding conjunctly in the same direction, demands of both conductor and singer utmost care for correct intonation.

With Expressionism and the succeeding Neo-classic movement harmonic experimentation is continued. The demarcation between dissonance and consonance disappears. Dissonance is cultivated for its own sake, for the interest which it can add to the chord as a whole. It is explored for the coloristic possibilities which it may possess as an element of the harmonic palette. Further, not only is it cultivated in its own right, the demand for its resolution is now removed.

The harmonic experimentations of the expressionists have come under the denomination of "atonality." The logic of this term is one debated by musicologists, and no exact, clear definition of it has been universally accepted. The strict meaning of the word would imply absence of tonal relationships. Accordingly, the term is in reality a misnomer, since some sort of relationship is unavoidably established between the individual members of the tonal group by the very fact of their employment in succession. However, the term properly may be taken to mean the absence of an established key or of established key relationships. In its denial of the traditional principles of chord construction and relation and of the principle of tonality as previously understood, such music may be properly called atonal, although Schoenberg himself refused to accept the label of atonality.

The twelve-tone system evolved by Schoenberg is an example of the changing concept of the period regarding the principles of harmonic and contrapuntal structure. Briefly, it may be described as a system in which the composer manipulates the tools mentioned on page 169 (melodic configurations, harmonic combinations, rhythmic motives) in the course of working and reworking, both successively and simultaneously, the elements of a set, that is, of a predetermined arrangement of the twelve tones within an octave, all the tones being treated as equals so that none lords it over the others, as does the tonic in music written in conventional major and minor. Preoccupation with experimentation of this type demonstrates the growing concern of the twentieth century with problems of construction. A similar preoccupation is evident in the Neo-classicism of the 1920's. For further discussion of the topic, reference is made to the articles "Atonality" and "Twelve-tone technique" in the *Harvard Dictionary of Music* and to Chapter VI of *Music Here and Now* by Ernst Křenek.[38]

With the Neo-classicism of the 1920's counterpoint perhaps becomes an even more important element of the structure. Harmonic concentration such as was evident in Impres-

---

38 Transl. Barthold Fles, New York, W. W. Norton, 1939.

sionism tends to produce a slowing down in the matter of progressional relationships. Concern with one chord as such, with the exploitation of the possibilities of one harmonic entity, inevitably detracts from linear movement. The emphasis on counterpoint brings one back to a linear conception.

The new counterpoint is in fact known as "linear" or "dissonant" in contradistinction to the counterpoint of previous periods, especially that of the Renaissance, which was based upon a theory of consonance between intervals, just as later counterpoint was based upon harmonic agreement. The dissonant counterpoint of the twentieth century recognizes no such restrictions. The contrapuntal lines are free to operate without reference to the exact manner of their combination, thus frequently producing dissonant clashes.

This development is of the greatest importance for the conductor of twentieth-century music. The music of Hindemith, for example, must be sung in such a way that the fluid quality of the individual line is maintained. There must be a sense of forward thrust in each voice. This does not mean that harmony does not result, but it does mean that the first aim of the conductor is to secure a clean, sharply engraved linear design with the harmony produced coincidentally, somewhat as in the music of the Renaissance, though in a strikingly different idiom.

c. Expressive quality of the score. The emotional statement of the impressionist is characterized by restraint of utterance. The extravagance of Romantic expression gives way to economy. The emotional line is drawn thinly, lacking in the broad sweep of the typical romanticist. The tone is clear and cool, detached as it were, attaining something of the classicist's survey of the scene from a point removed. The impressionist never becomes involved in the emotional whirlpool of the romanticist. The torrential stream of Romantic expression relaxes into a calm expanse in which the dramatic currents are reflected in a plastic movement rippling lightly on the surface.

The Expressionistic artist's approach results in a cer-

tain objectivity. What engages the artist's attention primarily
is not the actual representation of feeling but rather the
working out of a pattern originally initiated in the artist's
inner consciousness. The process takes on a quality of
intellectualism. It is removed by at least one step from the
direct mood representation of the romanticist. It is concerned
primarily with the manipulation of materials, though the
character of the manipulation is conditioned by the artist's
inner impulses. The expressionist seeks a reduction of the
personal element in building up the design.

Since the pattern as such is of primary importance rather
than the original emotional activity generating it, the interpretative artist will occupy himself first of all with a clear
delineation of the design of the work. He will not strive for
emotional representation in itself. What quality of expressiveness the performance yields must issue as a result of the
operation of the factors of the design upon the auditor's
own imaginative and emotional makeup.

This idea would presuppose that the emotional state
engendered by the Expressionistic work will not necessarily
be identical with that initiating the composition — unless, of
course, the auditor has such a complete understanding of
the artist's methods and vocabulary and is in such congeniality of spirit with him that he can enter into the same
emotional state. Whether it is the intention of Expressionism
to evoke such community of reaction is beyond the purpose
of this discussion. However, since mood representation is
not the primary aim, it is not to be the first concern of the
interpreter. Inasmuch as whatever emotional reaction takes
place is expected to occur as a result of the proper execution
of the design, the conductor must approach the performance
of the Expressionistic work with a sense of objectivity. The
intellectualism of Expressionism and the structural preoccupation of Neo-classicism both demand a reduction in
the expression of intimate personal feeling in favor of respect for structural elements.

    d. Dynamic scheme. The dynamic intensity of the romanticist disappears altogether from the Impressionistic score. The values themselves are greatly reduced. For the most part it is the middle and lower dynamic ranges that are employed — mezzo forte, piano, and pianissimo comprising the prevailing dynamic shades of the impressionist. Contrast is afforded through the use of forte and occasional fortissimos, but relatively little use is made of the upper dynamic extremes. Pianissimos, on the other hand, appear in profusion. A feeling of hushed suspension is created by the sighs and whispers of the lower extremes. Changes in dynamics are accomplished with the utmost delicacy. Crescendos and diminuendos demand the greatest subtlety in their application. Moderate changes, easy and gradual transitions from one level to another, frequent use of the lower extremes, a general dwelling within the middle and lower dynamic ranges, a customary avoidance of the higher intensities — these characterize the dynamic treatment of the typically Impressionistic work.

With Expressionism and Neo-classicism the leaning toward the excessively soft dynamic values is abandoned. There is a return to a conception of the normal dynamic range as lying around the middle degrees of intensity. At the same time, from Expressionism through Neo-classicism there is an increasing use of the dynamic extremes and of dynamic contrasts. As one approaches the present day more closely it is to be observed that the upper levels of the dynamic register are brought into play. Contrast is frequently obtained by the immediate juxtaposition of the lowest possible extremities of softness with the most terrific degrees of loudness.

As heretofore, the matter of dynamics is closely related to that of the sound ideal. There is in Expressionism and in Neo-classicism a tendency to abandon the large forces of late Romanticism in favor of a new economy of means and material. Interest shifts from the sonority of the large group to the combination of the individual timbres in the smaller ensemble. The chamber orchestra is utilized as one characteristic medium for the expression of the modern spirit; at the same time, twentieth-century musical practice continues to employ the larger symphonic body also. The particular coloristic possibilities of the specific instrument or voice are explored and extended. Timbre becomes, not as formerly an agent of expression, but rather one of the elements of the design, now often existing in its own right. The various shades of timbre within the particular medium are exploited for their own value without reference to emotional expression or dynamic nuance. Consequently, there is a trend toward the conception of dynamic values in terms of large areas of uniform color, rather than in terms of passages of graduated nuance.[39] As a result much modern music possesses a quality of dynamic flatness produced by the maintenance of one dynamic value over an extended period. When the value involved is one of high intensity, a cumulative effect of excitement is provided by the insistent repetition of the upper reaches of the dynamic register.

Characteristic of the twentieth-century style is variety in dynamic treatment. Flat levels of uniform intensity, violent dynamic accents, sudden and decided crescendos and diminuendos, high and low degrees of volume, all appear in music of the present day. Every known dynamic device is employed and exploited in the course of twentieth-century literature.

By way of summary, the following is to be noted:

a. *Meter and tempo.* Vigorous activity characterizes much contemporary music. Delight in sheer rhythm, joy in motion purely for the love of motion epitomize the modern spirit.

b. *Structural relationship between counterpoint and harmony.* Harmony is a prime consideration, with much use of dissonance, the flavor of which must be maintained with particularly accurate intonation. The driving effect of linear counterpoint is a salient feature of much of the best contemporary writing.

---

39 See article by Manfred F. Bukofzer, "The Neo-baroque," *Modern Music,* XXII (1945), 152-156.

c. Expressive quality of the score. Objectivity rather than subjectivity is the prevailing motto of twentieth-century Modernism, involving a reduction of the personal element as far as emotional expressiveness is concerned.

d. Dynamic scheme. The upper dynamic levels of contemporary music attain a degree of intensity not frequently encountered previously. Intensification of the dynamic power through percussive accentuation is a frequent procedure in twentieth-century music. Dynamic devices are multitudinous in number and variegated in effect.

In conclusion, it is to be observed that no single statement will hold for any one aspect of the music of the present day. The one generalization which must be maintained is that the music of the Modern period is characterized by variety in technique and effect, by lack of uniformity in method and style.

One of the most obvious features of twentieth-century writing is the experimental attitude brought about by the influence upon the musician of the spirit of investigation and the intellectual curiosity of the time. The scientific approach of the age has led to experimentation of all desscriptions. New chords and new harmonic relationships, new systems of harmony and new theories of scale building, new intervallic relationships are tried. New timbres and tonal colors are sought and explored. New combinations of instrumental and vocal color, new ideas of expression and nuance, new types of contrapuntal leadings, new treatments of dissonance and consonance, new concepts of structure are evolved. Experiment is the order of the day.

It may be remarked that in general the manner of statement tends toward conciseness and brevity. A cogent and terse thematic motive often serves as the germ of the typically modern work. An elimination of superfluities, a stripping down to the bare essentials is evident in a new simplicity of means and of utterance.

It is to be further observed that previously prevailing tendencies are found side by side with those which typify the essentially new mode of expression. Romanticism continues as a style in present-day writing. Impressionism exerts its influence long after Post-impressionistic tendencies have crystallized. Impressionism is heard in the twentieth century along with Futurism, Realism, Expressionism, and Neo-classicism.

He who would understand contemporary music must be aware, first of all, of the complexity of the skeins making up the pattern of the twentieth-century fabric. Only he can interpret twentieth-century music intelligently who knows the motives and techniques characteristic of the individual styles and the ways in which the various tendencies have found expression.

CHAPTER XVI

THE PERSONAL ELEMENT IN INTERPRETATION

To what extent should the personal attitude of the conductor enter into the interpretative scheme? Shall it be the composer's intention which formulates the performance style of a work? Or shall the work be re-created according to the conductor's own personal ideas? No categoric answer is to be found to either question. Rather, the reply will represent a fusion of the two concepts. The interpreter is to have respect for the composer's intention. That is basic to the work and is, after all, the final determinant of the finished form. But the interpreter has his contribution to make.

"Simplicity and directness" might well be taken as a motto for the aspiring conductor in determining the part he is to play in molding interpretative design. The approach should be one which attempts to reveal the fundamental content simply and without artifice. Let the conductor state the message of the composer directly and without the introduction of extravagant and extraneous effects. Nothing should be added to the music that will mar it; nothing superimposed that will draw attention to the performance of the work rather than to the work itself. The decorative architectural device must never be so prominently displayed that it detracts from the beauty of the building as a whole. Similarly, the interpretative effect should never be so highly exploited that it becomes an object of regard in itself, leading the mind of the listener away from the composition as a unified musical entity, making of the composition a framework upon which to display a series of startling effects.

The composer is not a tyrant whose dictum is to be arbitrarily imposed, but neither is the conductor to be a capricious prima donna whose fundamental motive is self-glorification. Fidelity to the composer's intention is the first constituent of interpretation, or of expression as it is sometimes called. Fidelity alone, however, is not sufficient.

183

Expression, or interpretation, must represent more than adherence to a pre-established pattern, more than a slavish repetition of what has been handed down from someone else. It must contain an essentially creative element of the interpreter's own making, illuminating the subject with fresh light.

It is to the score itself that the interpreter must first look for the key that will unlock the secret of the composer's thought, not in what others have said of the man, not in the scholars' estimates of the merit of the work. Biographical and historical writings are of value, but only as secondary sources. All avenues must be explored in order to arrive at completeness of understanding: familiarity with the music, acquaintance with the man, knowledge of the historical period; but first as prime essential is intimacy with the music.

The work of art is a composite of many elements, and the performer must be cognizant of all of them. He must possess sufficient understanding of the technique and theory of music to comprehend the vocabulary in which the thought is expressed. Further, a work can be brought to life only by one who views with sympathy the characteristic thought patterns of the time. Understanding of the man and of the way in which his thought processes develop, acquaintance with the musical syntax, congeniality with the spirit of the day contribute to the comprehension of the music. Perception of the impact of historical and social movements upon the composer as a personality and upon his work as art, appreciation of the relation of the man to his historical period and his social scene round out the picture which the interpreter must envision if he is to re-create the work with sympathy and intelligence.

The student of conducting will not find in the repetition of the interpretative schemes of others the solution to his problem. The truly musical conductor will carve out his own path. His approach will not be based upon whimsical conceptions, however, but founded upon logical conclusions reached through careful study and serious deliberation. The interpretations of the great conductors are valuable in indicating various approaches which have been made to particular works. They are often provocative and stimulating. They are to be understood in each case, however, as constituting the essentially subjective viewpoint of one person, who has set forth the work in terms of his own interpretative style. They are not necessarily models of perfection to be reproduced *in toto*.

Caprice is of course to be avoided. Let the conductor not strive to be different; let him not seek to find a new, eccentric way of setting forth the work that will capture attention by its novelty. Subjectivity of interpretation can never be eliminated, nor should it be, for the subjective factor gives the individual interpretation its characteristic flavor. Subjectivity is to be kept in check, however, not allowed to range untrammeled.

Subjectivity is first of all necessary in translating the score. Determination of tempo, for instance, remains largely· a matter of subjective judgment, even with the technical exactitude of modern notation. Although certain limits are definable which the allegro and the andante, for example, may not logically exceed, still, who can say exactly how fast is allegro and how slow is adagio? Even within the definable limits considerable variation is possible, and, furthermore, men of different periods have not always given tempo terms the same shade of meaning. Each era translates these terms in accordance with its own conceptions. Sociocultural historians have made much of the fact that the sense of speed varies from age to age, which is to say that the men of a particular cultural epoch have a tendency to move at a characteristic pace. What seems a normal rate of motion in one historical period may seem quite a rapid one to people of another period, but slow to those of a third.

The concept of duration represented by note values also has varied from age to age. The quarter-note, the half-note, the whole-note have all been interpreted variously by different periods. As time has progressed from early days to the present a tendency is evident toward the representation of the basic pulse in ever diminishing valuations. The whole-note was in earlier days taken as the unit of value, that is, as the symbol of one basic pulse. The quarter-note — which today usually represents at least a one-pulse value — stood for a much shorter valuation, and the whole- and half-note frequently were used where now the quarter-note customarily would be employed. The result is that the singer would think of this music as moving at a slower pace than is proper, owing to the visual impression he would receive if he were to sing from an early manuscript or print. Actually, in current practical editions the note values are usually adjusted according to the present-day concept.

The matter of dynamic treatment always has been and undoubtedly always will be a matter for subjective judgment. One man's forte is another man's piano. What one person understands as fortissimo is determined by his knowledge or lack of knowledge of the nuance, sound ideal, and relative dynamic values of a particular period. It is further affected by his own temperamental conception of the degrees of loudness and softness. The dynamic treatment will not necessarily be invariable in successive performances even of one work under the same conductor. The acoustical properties of the room and the size of the group have an especially strong influence upon the dynamic scheme of the choral performance and, as a matter of fact, are not entirely unrelated to the matter of tempo relationships.

The skillful and artistic director will not be governed by hard and fast rules of tempo and dynamic treatment, but will modify the interpretation as the exigencies of circumstance and place demand. Such modification, of course, will never be so extreme that the work is taken out of character. The variation which is employed not only will be dictated by circumstance and place, but also will be circumscribed by the nature and quality of the style of the work.

And so with all the elements of the score: time measurement, tempo modification, dynamic scheme, interrelation of contrapuntal parts, relationship between melodic and harmonic elements, relative treatment of dissonance, not to mention most obviously the portrayal of human emotion and dramatic conflict — all these depend upon the individual judgment of the interpreter. How necessary then that the conductor have as complete a knowledge as he is able to acquire of the technique and structure of music, of the concepts and the technical equipment of the composer, of the reaction of the composer to his historical and social background, of the characteristic thought-forms and modes of expression of the various historic periods. Above all, how important that he know the music thoroughly, that he have studied it, lived it, so absorbed it that he brings to it a creative contribution of his own, produced in the light of the composer's intent and the customs of the period.

BIBLIOGRAPHY

Abraham, Gerald. *A Hundred Years of Music*, London, Duckworth, 1938.

Abraham, Gerald. *Studies in Russian Music*, New York, Scribner's, 1936.

Adler, Guido. *Der Stil in der Musik.* I. Buch, "Prinzipien und Arten des musikalischen Stils." Leipzig, Breitkopf und Härtel, 1911.

Adler, Guido.. "Haydn and the Viennese Classical School," transl. W.O.Strunk, *Musical Quarterly*, XVIII (1932), 191-207.

Adler, Guido. "Style-Criticism," transl. W.O. Strunk, *Musical Quarterly*, XX (1934), 172-176.

Aldrich, Putnam. *Ornamentation in Bach's Organ Works*, New York, Coleman-Ross, 1950.

Apel, Willi, ed. *Harvard Dictionary of Music*, Cambridge, Mass., Harvard University Press, 1945.

Apel, Willi. *The Notation of Polyphonic Music*, Cambridge, Mass., Mediaeval Academy of America, 1942, 3rd corrected ed., 1944.

Allen, Warren D. *Philosophies of Music History*, New York, American Book Co., 1939.

Baker, Theodore. *A Dictionary of Musical Terms*, New York, G. Schirmer, 3rd ed., 1897, cop. 1895; 4th ed., 1940; Supplement, 1949.

Barrère, Georges. "Expression Unconfined," *Musical Quarterly*, XXX (1944), 192-197.

Bauer, Marion. *Twentieth Century Music,* New York, Putnam's, 6th impression, 1933.

Belaiev, Victor. "The Signs of Style in Music," transl. S.W. Pring, *Musical Quarterly,* XVI (1930), 366-377.

Blitzstein, Marc. "Towards a New Form," *Musical Quarterly,* XX (1934), 213-218.

Boyd, Morrison Comegys. *Elizabethan Music and Musical Criticism,* Philadelphia, University of Pennsylvania Press, 1940.

Bukofzer, Manfred. *Music in the Baroque Era: From Monteverdi to Bach,* New York, W. W. Norton, 1947.

Bukofzer, Manfred. "The Neo-baroque," *Modern Music,* XXII (1945), 152-156.

Bukofzer, Manfred. "On the Performance of Renaissance Music," *MTNA Proceedings,* XXXVI (1941), 225-235.

Brahms, Johannes. *A German Requiem,* New York, G. Schirmer.

Calvocoressi, M. D. *A Survey of Russian Music,* New York, Penguin Books, 1944.

Chanler, Theodore. "Rhythm and Habit," *Modern Music,* XXI (1944), 208-211.

Coeuroy, André. "The Esthetics of Contemporary Music," *Musical Quarterly,* XV (1929), 246-267.

Dahms, Walter. "Ihe 'Gallant' Style of Music," transl. Theodore Baker, *Musical Quarterly,* XI (1925), 356-372.

Davison, Archibald T. *Choral Conducting,* Cambridge, Mass., Harvard University Press, 1940.

Dannreuther, Edward. *Musical Ornamentation*, 2 vols., New York, Novello, Ewer, cop. 1893-95.

Deas, James. "The Limits of Expression," *Music and Letters*, XIII (1932), 418-420.

Dent, Edward J. "The Romantic Spirit in Music," *Musical Association Proceedings*, 59th session (1932-33), 85-102.

Dickinson, George Sherman. "The Study of Style as the Clue to Higher Music Education," *MTNA Proceedings*, XXXVIII (1944), 200-215.

Dolmetsch, Arnold. *The Interpretation of the Music of the XVIIth and XVIIIth Centuries*, London, Novello, 1915.

Dorian, Frederick. *The History of Music in Performance*, New York, W. W. Norton, 1942.

Dyson, George. *The New Music*, London, Oxford, 2nd ed. (1st ed., 1924).

Eckermann, J. P. *Conversations of Goethe with Eckermann and Soret*, transl. John Oxenford, London, George Bell, 1892, rev. ed.

Einstein, Alfred. *Music in the Romantic Era*, New York, W. W. Norton, 1947.

Ferguson, Donald. *A History of Musical Thought*, New York, Crofts, 1939.

Finney, Theodore. *A History of Music*, New York, Harcourt, Brace, 1935.

Forster, E.M. "On Criticism in the Arts, Especially Music," *Harper's Magazine*, July 1947, vol. 195, no. 1166, pp. 9-17.

Fuller Maitland, J.A. *The Consort of Music: A Study of Interpretation and Ensemble*, Oxford, Clarendon Press, 1915.

Fellowes, E. H. *The English Madrigal*, London, Oxford University Press, 1925.

Fellowes, E. H. *The English Madrigal Composers*, Oxford, Clarendon Press, 1921.

Friedell, Egon. *A Cultural History of the Modern Age*, transl. Charles Francis Atkinson, 3 vols., New York, Alfred A. Knopf, 1933.

Gastoué, Amédée. *Les Primitifs de la Musique Française*, Paris, Librairie Renouard, 1922.

Gatti, Guido M. "On the Interpretation of Music," transl. Henry Furst, *Musical Quarterly*, XVII (1931), 195-203.

Goodrich, Alfred J. *Complete Musical Analysis*, Cincinnati, John Church, 1889.

Goodrich, Alfred J. *Theory of Interpretation*, Philadelphia, Presser, 1899.

Gradenwitz, Peter. "Mid-Eighteenth-Century Transformations of Style," *Music and Letters*, XVIII (1937), 265-275.

Gray, Cecil. *A Survey of Contemporary Music*, London, Oxford University Press, 1924.

Greene, Harry Plunkett. *Interpretation in Song*, New York, Macmillan, 1912.

Grove's Dictionary of Music and Musicians, 5th ed., 9 vols., London, Macmillan, 1954.

Hadow, W. H. *Studies in Modern Music*, 2nd series, 12th ed., New York, Macmillan, 1935.

Haggin, B. H. "Music," *The Nation*, December 6, 1947, vol. 165, no. 23, pp. 630-631.

Harding, Rosamond E. M. *Origins of Musical Time and Expression*, London, Oxford University Press, 1938.

Haydon, Glen. "Musicology and Performance," *MTNA Proceedings*, XXXV (1940), 80-87.

Helm, Everett B. "The Sixteenth Century French Chanson," *MTNA Proceedings*, XXXVI (1941), 236-243.

Henderson, W. J. *Early History of Singing*, New York, Longmans, Green, 1921.

Henderson, W. J. *The Art of the Singer*, New York, Scribner's, 1906.

Hibberd, Lloyd. "On 'Instrumental' Style in Early Melody," *Musical Quarterly*, XXXII (1946), 107-130.

Hull, A Eaglefield. *Music: Classical, Romantic and Modern*, New York, Dutton, 1927.

Jarosy, A. "Emotion in Performance," *Musical Quarterly*, XVII (1936), 54-58.

Křenek, Ernst. *Music Here and Now*, transl. Barthold Fles, New York, W. W. Norton, 1939.

Lambert, Constant. *Music Ho! A Study of Music in Decline*, New York, Scribner's, 1934.

Landowska, Wanda. *Music of the Past*, transl. W. A. Bradley, New York, Alfred A. Knopf, 1924.

Lang, Paul Henry. *Music in Western Civilization*, New York, W. W. Norton, 1941.

Lang, Paul Henry. "The So-called Netherlands Schools," *Musical Quarterly*, XXV (1939), 48-59.

Langley, George. "Musical Expression from the Performer's Point of View," *Musical Association Proceedings*, 38th session (1911-12), 1-20.

Latham, Peter. "The Score—Servant or Master?" *Music and Letters*, XXV (1944), 33-45.

Leichtentritt, Hugo. *Music, History, and Ideas*, Cambridge, Mass., Harvard University Press, 8th printing, 1947.

Lourié, Arthur. "The Russian School," *Musical Quarterly*, XVIII (1932), 519-529.

Lussy, Mathis. *Traité de l'Expression Musicale*, Paris, Heugel, 1874.

Mason, Daniel Gregory. *The Romantic Composers*, NewYork, Macmillan, 1906.

Manziarly, Marcelle de. "On Rhythm, Complex and Simple," *Modern Music*, XXI (1944), 70-75.

Matthay, Tobias. *Musical Interpretation*, Boston, Boston Music Co., 5th ed., 1913.

McKinney, Howard D. and W. R. Anderson. *Music in History: The Evolution of an Art*, New York, American Book Co., 1940.

Mees, Arthur. *Choirs and Choral Music*, New York, Scribner's, 1901.

Mendl, R. W. S. "Performance," *Musical Quarterly*, X (1924), 532-545.

Moore, Douglas. *From Madrigal to Modern Music*, New York, W. W. Norton, 1942.

194

Morris, R. O. *Contrapuntal Technique in the Sixteenth Century*, Oxford, Clarendon Press, 1922.

Morley, Thomas. *A Plaine and Easie Introduction to Practicall Musicke*, London, 1597.

Motta, J. Vianna da. "Zur Pflege der Bachschen Klavierwerke," *Neue Zeitschrift für Musik,* 71. Jahrgang, no. 40, 28. September, 1904, 678-680.

Newman, Ernest. "Interpretation," *The International Cyclopedia of Music and Musicians,* New York, Dodd, Mead, 5th ed., 1949.

Ohl, John F. *The Orchestration of Bach's Vocal Works,* 4 vols., Ph. D. Thesis, Harvard University, Cambridge, Mass., 1943.

Parker, D. C.. "Music and the Grand Style," *Musical Quarterly,* VIII (1922), 161-179.

Parkhurst, Helen Huss. *Cathedral: A Gothic Pilgrimage,* Boston, Houghton, Mifflin, 1936.

Parry, C. H. H. *Johann Sebastian Bach,* New York, Putnam's, 1909.

Parry, C. H. H. *Style in Musical Art,* London, Macmillan, 1911.

Praeger, Ferdinand. "Style," *Musical Association Proceedings,* 12th session (1885-86), 91-105.

Pratt, Waldo Selden. *The New Encyclopedia of Music and Musicians,* New York, Macmillan, 1924.

Prunières, Henry. *Monteverdi: His Life and Work,* transl. Marie D. Mackie, London and Toronto, Dent, 1926.

Radcliffe, Philip F. "The Relation of Rhythm and Tonality in the 16th Century," *Musical Association Proceedings,* 57th session (1930-31), 73-97.

Reese, Gustave. *Music in the Middle Ages*, New York, W. W. Norton, 1940.

Reese, Gustave. *Music in the Renaissance*, New York, W. W. Norton, 1954.

Riemann, Hugo. *Riemanns Musik-Lexikon*, Elfte Aufl., 2 vols., Berlin, Hesse, 1929.

Rosenwald, Hans. "Changes in the Approach to Bach," *MTNA Proceedings*, XXXIV (1939), 215-228.

Salazar, Adolfo. *Music in Our Time*, transl. Isabel Pope, New York, W. W. Norton, 1946.

Schweitzer, Albert. *J. S. Bach*, 2 vols., transl. Ernest Newman, Leipzig, Breitkopf und Härtel, 1911.

Scott, Charles Kennedy. *Madrigal Singing*, London, Oxford, 1st ed., 1907; 2nd ed., 1931.

Scott, Charles Kennedy. "Some Thoughts on Polyphonic Rhythm," *Musical Association Proceedings*, 37th session (1910-11), 29-63.

Sorantin, Erich. *The Problem of Musical Expression*, Nashville, Tenn., Marshall and Bruce, 1932.

Spitta, Philipp. *Johann Sebastian Bach*, transl. Clara Bell and J. A. Fuller Maitland, 3 vols., London, Novello, Ewer, 1885.

Stainer, John and W. A. Barrett. *A Dictionary of Musical Terms*, New York, Novello, 3rd ed., pref. dated 1888.

Stanford, Charles Villiers. *Interludes*, London, Murray, 1922.

Terry, Charles S. *Bach's Orchestra*, London, Oxford University Press, 1932.

Terry, Charles S. *The Music of Bach*, London, Oxford University Press, 1933.

Thomas, Kurt. *Lehrbuch der Chorleitung*, Leipzig, Breitkopf und Härtel, 1939-40.

Thompson, Oscar, ed. *The International Cyclopedia of Music and Musicians*, New York, Dodd, Mead, 5th ed., 1949.

Tiersot, Julien. "Music and the Centenary of Romanticism," transl. Frederick H. Martens, *Musical Quarterly*, XV (1929), 268-280.

Tovey, Donald Francis. *Essays in Musical Analysis*, 6 vols., London, Oxford University Press, 1935-39.

Tovey, Donald Francis. *Musical Textures* (A Musician Talks, vol. II), London, Oxford University Press, 1941.

Tovey, Donald Francis. "The Training of the Musical Imagination," *Music and Letters*, XVII (1936), 337-356.

Turner, E. O. "The Interpretation of Music: A Theory of Communication," *Musical Quarterly*, XXX (1944), 297-306.

Verdi, Giuseppe. *Manzoni Requiem*, Milan, London, Ricordi.

Warlock, Peter, pseud. for Philip Heseltine. *The English Ayre*, London, Milford, 1926.

Webster's New International Dictionary of the English Language, 2nd ed., unabridged, Springfield, Mass., Merriam, 1947, cop. 1945.

Weissmann, Adolf. *Der Dirigent im 20. Jahrhundert*, Berlin, Propyläenverlag, 1925.

Weissmann, Adolf. *The Problems of Modern Music*, New York, Dutton, 1925.

Whittaker, W. G. *Fugitive Notes on Certain Cantatas and the Motets of J. S. Bach*, London, Oxford University Press, 1924.

Whittaker, W. G. "A Pilgrimage through the Church Cantatas of J. S. Bach," *Collected Essays*, London, Oxford University Press, 1940.

Whittaker, W. G. "Some Problems in the Performance of Bach's Church Cantatas," *Musical Association Proceedings*, 54th session (1927-28), 35-61.

Wodell, Frederick W. *Choir and Chorus Conducting*, Philadelphia, Presser, 1901.

Wood, R. W. "Putting in the Expression," *Music and Letters*, XI (1930), 375-382.

Woodworth, G. Wallace. "The Performance of Bach: An Example of the Relation between Research and Practical Music-making," Reprint from paper for AMS, Pittsburgh, Pa., December 29-30, 1937.

INDEX

198